Ancient Civilizations
READER'S THEATER
DEVELOP READING FLUENCY AND TEXT COMPREHENSION SKILLS

Written by
Deborah Ellermeyer and Judy Rowell

To my children, Anna and James Ellermeyer, for their love and support. ~DAE

To my parents, Tobia and Aurora Schinella, teachers of love and learning. ~JSR

Editor: Alaska Hults
Illustrator: Corbin Hillam
Cover Illustrator: Amy Vangsgard
Designer: Jane Wong-Saunders
Cover Designer: Barbara Peterson
Art Director: Tom Cochrane
Project Director: Carolea Williams

Table of Contents

6 = total number of parts

INTRODUCTION

Fluency instruction provides a bridge between being able to "read" a text and being able to understand it. Readers who decode word by word sound plodding and choppy. They are too busy figuring out the words to think about what they are reading. Fluent readers are accurate, quick, and able to read with expression. They make the reading sound interesting. Beyond the experience of the listener, fluent readers are also demonstrating skills that are crucial to their understanding of what they read. Fluent readers recognize words at a glance, group words into meaningful phrases, and move beyond the struggle to decode individual words. They are able to focus on making sense of what they read.

Reader's Theater is an exciting way to help students improve reading fluency without being too time intensive for the teacher. It requires no props and no additional teaching skills on your part, and it is not difficult to manage. Reader's Theater promotes better reading comprehension because students who have learned to read a passage expressively also come to better understand its meaning. In addition, research says that these gains transfer well to new text. Reader's Theater also addresses standards in listening while providing a fun environment for everyone involved. When students practice their lines, they read and reread the same passages. Under your direction, they gradually add more expression, read more smoothly, and find any subtle meanings in the passages.

The scripts in *Ancient Civilizations Reader's Theater* are intended to be read in large groups of 6 to 13 students. Each script is prefaced by an activity that focuses on vocabulary from the script, the factual and fictional background of the piece, fluency instruction specific to that script, and comprehension questions that span the levels of Bloom's Taxonomy. Each script is followed by one or two whole-class activities related to the content of the script.

These scripts are designed for fluency instruction. While they are based on factual information about the time period or characters, many of the characters and scenes are entirely fictional. The overall purpose is to provide students with text at their reading level that is fun to read. The background section that precedes each script provides additional information about the characters or the period around which the script is built. All the scripts provide the following hallmarks of a good Reader's Theater text:

• fast-moving dialogue
• action
• humor
• narrative parts

Ancient Civilizations Reader's Theater provides hours of fluency practice that is grounded in the familiar format of ancient history. The large-group format gives students an opportunity to work together to craft an entertaining reading for a peer or adult audience.

How To Use This Book

Each Reader's Theater script should be covered over the course of five practice days (although those days do not need to be consecutive). The first day should include some or all of the elements of the suggested reading instruction. It should also include an expressive reading by you of the script as students read along silently. On each of the following days, give students an opportunity to practice their reading. On the final day, have each group read its script for the class.

Five sections that support reading instruction precede each script. You will find **vocabulary, background information** for the script, **a brief description of each character,** specific **coaching for fluency instruction,** and **comprehension questions** that progress from the simplest level of understanding to the most complex.

On the first day of instruction, briefly discuss with students the vocabulary. Each vocabulary list includes a short activity to help students understand the meaning of each vocabulary word. For example, the vocabulary activity for The Aztecs (page 7) asks students to pantomime the words.

Next, use the background and information about each character to tell students what the script will be about and describe the characters.

Read aloud the script, modeling clear enunciation and a storyteller's voice. Do not be afraid to exaggerate your expression—it will hold the attention of your audience and stick more firmly in their minds when they attempt to mimic you later. Model the pacing you expect from them as they read.

Finish the reading instruction by discussing the fluency tips with students and having them answer the questions in the comprehension section.

Now it is time to give students a copy of the script! Use the following schedule of student practice for a five-day instruction period.

Day 1	After following the steps outlined on page 4, give each student a personal copy of the script. Pair students and have Partner A read all the parts on the first page, Partner B read all the parts on the second page, and so on.
Days 2 and 3	Assign students to a group. Give each group a script for each student, and have each student highlight a different part. Have students gather to read aloud the script as many times as time permits. Have them change roles with each reading by exchanging the highlighted scripts. Move from group to group, providing feedback and additional modeling as needed. At the *end* of day 3, assign roles or have students agree on a role to own.

Day 4	Have each group read aloud the script. Move from group to group and provide feedback. Have students discuss their favorite lines at the end of each reading and why the manner in which they are read works well. Repeat.
Day 5	Have each group perform its script for the rest of the class (or other audience members provided by buddy classes and/or school personnel).

Throughout the week, or as time permits, provide students with the activity or activities that follow each script. These are optional and do not have to be completed to provide fluency instruction; however, many provide students with additional background information that may help them better understand the characters or setting of the script.

Additional Tips

- Use the Reader's Theater Planning reproducible (page 6) to track the assigned roles for each group and to jot down any informal observations you make for assessment. Use these observations to drive future fluency instruction.

- Notice that there are no staging directions in the scripts. These plays are written to be read expressively in a storyteller's voice. If the focus is placed on *acting out* the script, students will shift their focus from the reading to the movement. If students become enchanted with a script and want to act it out, invite them to do so after they have mastered the reading. Then, have the group go through the script and brainstorm their own staging directions to jot in the margins.

- To fit fluency instruction into an already full day of instruction, it will work best to have all groups work on the same script. This will permit you to complete the first day's activities as a whole class. Students will enjoy hearing how another child reads the same lines, and some mild competition to read expressively will only foster additional effort.

- If you have too many roles for the number of students in a group, assign one child more than one part.

- If you have too many students for parts, divide up the narrator parts. As a rule, these parts tend to have longer lines.

- The roles with the greatest and least number of words to read are noted in the teacher pages. The ⬆ and ⬇ indicate a higher or lower *word count*. They are not a reflection of reading level. The narrator parts usually reflect the highest reading level. However, less fluent readers may benefit from having fewer words to master. More advanced readers may benefit from the challenge of the greater word count.

Reader's Theater Planning

Group 1		Script: _____
Name	**Part**	**Notes:**

Group 2		Script: _____
Name	**Part**	**Notes:**

Group 3		Script: _____
Name	**Part**	**Notes:**

Ancient Civilizations Reader's Theater © 2004 Creative Teaching Press

THE AZTECS

ANCIENT
CIVILIZATIONS

VOCABULARY

Discuss each of the following words with students. Then, have volunteers pantomime the words, and invite the rest of the class to identify the word.

amaranth: a plant with dark green or reddish clusters of tiny flowers used in cooking

cacao: a tropical tree whose seeds are used in making chocolate, cocoa, and cocoa butter

glyphs: symbols used for writing

labret: a piece of wood, shell, or stone worn in a perforation of the lip or cheek

macaw: a kind of parrot found in Central and South America that has a long tail, a curved, powerful bill, and usually brilliant feathers

quetzal: a Central American bird that has brightly colored bronze-green and red feathers

ulama: an Aztec ball game played with two teams that was similar to soccer and basketball

BACKGROUND

The Aztecs came to present-day Mexico and Latin America from the north about A.D. 1300. Their empire included as many as 15 million people living in 500 towns and cities. Huey Tlatoani was an Aztec leader, the Great Speaker, but his family and preparations for his naming day celebration were invented for this play. In A.D. 1519, the Spaniards conquered the Aztec people, their land, and the last Aztec emperor, Montezuma II, through warfare and diseases. Nahuatl, the oral language used by the Aztecs, is still spoken in some remote areas of Mexico.

In this play, Tetl and Calli's city is based on Tenochtitlan, the government center of the Aztecs. Three times a week, market-day vendors spread their wares on reed mats in the market square. There were over 400 more permanent shops in the streets around the market. A trip to the market was time-consuming yet productive in locating needed goods and news. For food the Aztecs raised dogs and turkeys, and they hunted for rabbits, waterfowl, fish, deer, and armadillos. They ate maize, beans, squash, grasshoppers, locusts, insect eggs, cactus worms, chili peppers, tomatoes, and amaranth porridge.

There were several kinds of Aztec scribes who recorded different events. In this play, Father is a general scribe, who makes books out of strips of deer skin, uses pictograms and glyphs, and folds the strips like an accordion. Only a few of these books, called codices, survived Spanish destruction.

Because about half of their children died by the age of 5, the Aztecs developed customs to ensure babies had the best advantages to survive. Readings of sacred calendars by astrologers for "lucky" names and days for naming celebrations and special gifts were ways a family could prepare a healthy life for an infant. Even though illness was thought to be caused by evil spirits, the Aztecs could set broken bones, suture cuts, and prescribe healing herbs, seeds, roots, leaves, minerals, and nuts to cure illness or to relieve symptoms.

PARTS

Narrator 1

Narrator 2

Anilama (honored elder): Calli's and Tetl's grandmother

Tetl (stone): 9-year-old brother of Calli

Calli (house): 10-year-old sister of Tetl

Father: chief scribe of the city and father of Calli and Tetl

Papalotl (butterfly): nicknamed "Pap," a helpful 9-year-old girl

Astrologer: Papalotl's father

Nezahual Coyotl (hungry coyote): nicknamed "Nezzie," an 11-year-old girl

Chapultepec (grasshopper hill): nicknamed "Chap," a 10-year-old boy

Cautla (forest): a 12-year-old boy

Feathermaker

FLUENCY INSTRUCTION

Have students discuss the ages of the characters to help them reflect the maturity level in their reading. When you read aloud the script for students, have them listen for the following:

- The pace of the reading helps show the level of the speaker's excitement. Read aloud the lines **Anilama:** *Wake up, Tetl and Calli! It is a beautiful, wonderful day! A special day!* and **Tetl:** *[yawning] Grandmother, it is still dark out!* Have students notice that Anilama's lines are read at a slightly faster pace. She already knows there is exciting news of a new birth. Tetl has just woken from a deep sleep and does not know there is anything to be excited about yet.

- Calli and Tetl's father is older than the children in the play, but his age is not given. Have students estimate the age of the father and demonstrate how his voice would be different than the voice of 9-year-old Tetl.

- Commas signal a pause. Reread the line **Anilama:** *By yourselves. When you return, I'll decide if I should have trusted you.* Have students read this line in two ways: pausing at the comma and without pausing. Ask them to explain how the comma helps communicate the meaning of the sentence.

COMPREHENSION

After you read aloud the script, ask students these questions:

1. What is the good news that Anilama shares with Calli and Tetl?

2. How did Calli and Tetl feel when Anilama told them they would go to the market-place alone? How would you feel?

3. What part did each of the following people play in the Aztec culture: chief scribe, astrologer, healer, and feathermaker? Identify three important people/jobs in your culture.

4. Do you think that Tetl and Calli selected a good gift for Tepito? Explain why or why not.

5. Think about a special occasion that you celebrate with your family. Tell how your family prepares for the celebration.

A SPECIAL DAY

PARTS

Narrator 1
Narrator 2
Anilama (honored elder): Calli's and
     Tetl's grandmother
Tetl (stone): 9-year-old brother of Calli
Calli (house): 10-year-old sister of Tetl
Father: chief scribe of the city and
     father of Calli and Tetl
Papalotl (butterfly): nicknamed "Pap,"
     a helpful 9-year-old girl
Astrologer: Papalotl's father
Nezahual Coyotl (hungry coyote):
     nicknamed "Nezzie," an 11-year-old girl
Chapultepec (grasshopper hill):
     nicknamed "Chap," a 10-year-old boy
Cautla (forest): a 12-year-old boy
Feathermaker

Narrator 1: Before the dawn of a new day greets the Aztec city, Anilama wakes Tetl and Calli with good news and a list of tasks for the day.

Anilama: Wake up, Tetl and Calli! It is a beautiful, wonderful day! A special day!

Tetl: [yawning] Grandmother, it is still dark out!

Calli: Beautiful? Wonderful? Special? What are you trying to tell us, Grandmother?

Father: Anilama is telling you that your new baby brother was born during the night!

Calli: Why didn't you say so? What's his name? Can we see him and Mother?

Father: You will see them later. We must make plans for his naming day.

Anilama: We shall call him Tepito, Little One, until we have his naming celebration.

Tetl: I will teach him to play ulama! That will build strong muscles!

Father: Tetl, you'll be a big help—someday! But no ball games yet!

Calli: How can we help, Grandmother?

Anilama: Today you'll go to the marketplace and shops to buy what we need for Tepito's naming celebration.

Calli and Tetl: By ourselves? You trust us?

Anilama: By yourselves. When you return, I'll decide if I should have trusted you.

Calli: Ummm. What happens if you think that you should not have trusted us?

Father: Your names say it all.

A Special Day

Tetl:	Our names? Mine means "stone" and Calli's means "house."
Calli:	Are you saying that Tetl will be turned to stone and I will stay in the house?
Anilama:	We'll see.
Tetl:	We have never been to the marketplace and shops alone!
Anilama:	You must learn sometime. At 9 and 10 years old, the time is now!
Calli:	Oh, dear. What do we do?
Father:	The detailed glyphs, next to each item, will help.
Tetl:	With over 400 shops in our city center, this list will take us all day!
Anilama:	We agree, Tetl! All day! Now come to the fireplace for a bowl of amaranth, which will fill you until our evening meal.
Calli:	How will we pay the shopkeepers?
Anilama:	I have packed the woven market bag with my colorful weavings. You'll have no trouble exchanging my items for the shopkeepers' goods.
Narrator 2:	Calli puts Anilama's woven bag over her shoulder. They step outside into the first streaks of daylight. The air is cool, but not for long.
Father:	On your way to the market, please stop at the astrologer's shop. Ask him to come after he checks the calendars and decides on Tepito's name and day for naming. That is one way we can help Tepito grow well and strong.
Calli:	Yes, Father. Will you be in your shop making a book for Tepito?
Father:	Yes. I will see you later.
Narrator 1:	Calli and Tetl walk toward the marketplace while reading Anilama's list. They greet their friend Papalotl, who is helping her father, the astrologer.
Astrologer:	Welcome Calli and Tetl. How can I help you this morning?
Calli:	Our new baby brother, Tepito, arrived. Father asked if you could visit.
Astrologer:	Of course! The calendars will decide on the best name and naming day for your brother. I will check the placement of the sun, stars, and planets.
Tetl:	Thank you. We are off now. Anilama trusts us to shop for her.
Calli:	Tetl and I must find a gift for Tepito as well.

Ancient Civilizations Reader's Theater © 2004 Creative Teaching Press

A Special Day

Pap: Father, could I help Tetl and Calli?

Astrologer: Go ahead. If you go near the healer's tent, buy a root of the Rabbit Fern for my stiff knees.

Narrator 2: The children walk into the exciting, lively marketplace, which is several blocks long. The sellers have set up their wares on large reed mats.

Pap: Your gift for Tepito is important for his future. What are your ideas?

Tetl: How about an ulama rubber ball?

Calli: No! No! No! Playing ulama is dangerous! Ummm. How about a digging stick for the garden? It loosens the earth and helps to harvest the foods.

Tetl: No! No! No! He would be outside every day in all kinds of weather.

Pap: Here we are at Vegetable Alley. And here's Nezzie coming from the fields.

Pap, Tetl, and Calli: Hi, Nezzie!

Tetl and Calli: We're here to buy food for our new brother's naming celebration!

Tetl: We need avocados, prickly pears, beans, chilies, and squash for a stew.

Nezzie: Special food for a special day. I'll carry the food home for you. We have something new, peanuts, brought back from the south by traders.

Pap: How do you use peanuts?

Nezzie: They're good cooked or uncooked. Try mother's peanut soup.

Calli: [sipping soup] Yummy! If your mother shares her recipe, we'll buy some peanuts.

Tetl: Nezzie, thanks for helping! Now we must find a new cooking pot!

Narrator 1: Nezzie loads a bag with fresh vegetables and fruit. Her mother is glad to share her recipe and to have a new piece of excellent weaving. The children turn into the potter's corner where there are pots of all shapes and sizes.

Calli: Wow! Tetl, maybe we'll find a gift here for Tepito.

Tetl: Remember my naming pot? I had it for 7 years. Seven years!

Calli and Pap: We remember! You scared us out of our skins!

Tetl: You? What about me? When I reached into my pot and felt skin cool, smooth, but definitely alive, I didn't even think. I threw it . . . well, you know the rest.

Nezzie: Yes, "Crash!" That frightened king snake slithered quickly outside!

Pap: It wanted a dark place to sleep and to digest its lizard lunch. What a way to wake up!

Tetl: I won't be giving Tepito a clay pot! I don't want him to be in danger!

Calli: You weren't in danger, Tetl. You were more dangerous than the snake.

Nezzie: Here's Chap!

Everyone (except Chap): Hi, Chap! What's new?

Chap: Mother made a new cooking pot for several hundred grasshoppers. You add hoppers, water, and herbs. Place it on the fire. The hoppers are ready in an hour. Delicious! Do you want a hopper pot?

Tetl: We do need a new stew pot for our baby brother's naming day . . .

Nezzie: Special day, special food, special cooking pot.

Chap: We have all kinds. Here's a great grasshopper pot. It has sturdy handles. It's easier to lift out of the fire.

Calli: It's the right size. I think Anilama will like the handles.

Chap: I'll carry it home for you. What's next on your list?

Calli: The gold and silver shop for a gold charm for Tepito.

Narrator 2: As the children pass the healers' tent, Pap stops for a root for her father. Dried herbs, flowers, cacti, leaves, roots, nuts, seeds, and snake skins are hanging in jars and pouches.

Cautla: Welcome, friends. Something for fever or cough? Leeches to help blood circulation?

Pap and Calli: Ugh! Please, no!

Pap: I need Rabbit Fern root for my father's stiff knees. Do you have any?

Tetl: Hey, Calli, let's find a present for Tepito! Bat wings? A cactus top?

Calli: Stop right there, Tetl. Think of Tepito's future.

Ancient Civilizations Reader's Theater © 2004 Creative Teaching Press

A SPECIAL DAY

Cautla: This Rabbit Fern root is very fresh. It will help your father, Pap. Calli, I'll come with you to give Anilama these fragrant herbs for the naming day tea!

Pap: Thanks, Cautla. Let's go! Calli and Tetl still have items on their list.

Narrator 1: As the friends make their way past the traders, the weavers, and spinners, Calli and Tetl continue to think about an appropriate gift for Tepito.

Calli: We need to find something beautiful, lasting, and powerful.

Tetl: A naming day gift will aid him in the future.

Chap: You will find the perfect gift in one of these many shops.

Calli: Here's the gold and silver shop where Anilama ordered a charm for Tepito.

Pap: She wants to make sure he is well protected.

Nezzie: A special day, special food, special pot, special tea, and special charm.

Tetl: We could get him a golden labret, Calli. A perfect gift.

Calli: A great idea, Tetl, but too expensive for us.

Narrator 2: In the shop, the jewelers are stringing long threads of gold for necklaces, earrings, bracelets, and labrets.

Narrator 1: After picking up Anilama's charm, the list is complete. Still they have not found a proper gift for Tepito.

Narrator 2: The children wander into another part of the city. Before them are hundreds of birds, all sizes and colors, cooing, cawing, squawking, and singing.

Pap: Where are we?

Feathermaker: You are in Feather Square.

Calli: What do you have?

Feathermaker: Feathers from ducks, turkeys, sharp-eyed birds like hawks and eagles, and shiny, iridescent feathers from birds like quetzals, macaws, and parrots.

Chaps: What do you make with all of those feathers?

Feathermaker: We make headdresses, necklaces, pillows, capes, fans, and many other helpful, beautiful things.

Ancient Civilizations Reader's Theater © 2004 Creative Teaching Press

A SPECIAL DAY

Tetl: Would you have anything for a new baby brother?

Feathermaker: I made a fan from feathers that hung over a baby's bed. When the baby was cranky and cross, the family tickled him with the feathers.

Calli: Did it break? Wear out? Was it dangerous?

Feathermaker: No. No. And no! Years later, when the baby was a strong teenager, he returned to have his feathers woven into an elaborate, sacred headdress.

Tetl and Calli: A sacred headdress?

Feathermaker: Yes. He is now our Great Speaker.

Tetl and Calli: Wow! So feathers can help direct a baby on his future path?

Feathermaker: Absolutely.

Tetl: How do we choose the right feathers for our brother?

Feathermaker: I know the powers and secret ways of feathers and birds. I'll help.

Narrator 2: After Feathermaker makes a beautiful fan for Tepito, Tetl's and Calli's friends carry everything back to the chief scribe's house.

Father: Welcome to all. Tell us about your day.

Nezzie: Special day, special food, special pot, special tea, special charm, and special gift.

Calli: Nezzie has summed it up.

Tetl: We have everything on the list, and we have new things to share with you!

Nezzie: Like peanuts and a recipe for peanut soup.

Chaps: Like a grasshopper pot that cooks hundreds at once.

Cautla: Like new herbs for naming day tea.

Father: Like a new codex covered with soft deer hide.

Pap: And a perfect gift for Tepito.

Tetl: A feather fan! It will amuse him now and help him as he grows.

Calli: Now, Anilama, have you decided whether you *should* trust us?

Tetl: Or will I be turned to stone and Calli held prisoner in the house?

Ancient Civilizations Reader's Theater © 2004 Creative Teaching Press

A SPECIAL DAY

Anilama: [laughing] I trusted you from the beginning. You are my trusted, honorable grandchildren. Now, would anyone like a cacao drink?

Nezzie: Special day, special food, special pot, special tea, special charm, special gift, and now—yummy—a special drink.

Calli: Don't forget: special friends.

Everyone: Special friends!

Narrator: The naming day celebration was a success with friends and family gathered to offer support and good wishes for a healthy and happy life. In years to follow, Tepito's official name, Huey Tlatoani, became known throughout the Aztec civilization as an honorable leader, the Great Speaker.

RELATED LESSON

It's More Than Just a Name

OBJECTIVE

Explore resource books and/or the Internet to discover the origin and meaning of individual student names and to interview parents and/or relatives to discover how and why their names were chosen.

ACTIVITY

Tell students that naming is very important in many cultures. It was celebrated with a special day within the Aztec culture. Aztec parents thoughtfully selected names for their children. With the help of **name reference books,** have students explore the origins and meanings of their own individual names. Encourage students to interview their parents, grandparents, or other family members to learn more about why they were given their names. Ask *Were you named after someone special in your family? Were you named after someone special in history?* Give each student a **My Name reproducible (page 17).** Have students glue their **baby picture** in the space indicated and complete the reproducible. Mount student information sheets on **colored construction paper,** and display them on a classroom or hall bulletin board titled *It's More Than Just a Name.* For added fun, have a naming day celebration, and invite students to share their name discoveries over a **cacao drink (chocolate milk).**

My Name

Attach or draw baby picture here.

My name is
I was born on
My name means
I was named by
I was given this name because
I feel _____ about my name because

Ancient Civilizations Reader's Theater © 2004 Creative Teaching Press

THE INCA

ANCIENT CIVILIZATIONS

VOCABULARY

Write each of the following words on a large index card, and place the cards in a bag. Discuss the meaning of each word. Then, ask a volunteer to randomly select three cards from the bag and place them on the board. Have a student select two of the words and identify one aspect that they have in common (e.g., meaning, part of speech, vowel sound). Finally, have the student define the third word. Replace the words in the bag and repeat.

alpaca: a South American animal, similar to a llama, which has long, fine, wooly hair

chasqui: an Inca runner

llama: a South American mammal, related to the camel, raised for its soft, fleecy wool and used as a work animal

Llikichiri: a scary fictional character in the Inca culture

quinoa: the high-protein dried fruits and seeds of a plant used in Chile and Peru, which is ground into flour and used in making porridge and cakes

terrace: a raised, flat, narrow stretch of ground

BACKGROUND

This play details the daily life of the people of the Inca Empire, who lived in the high altitudes of the Andes Mountains from A.D. 1438–1535, after which the Spanish arrived and the empire was overtaken. Today, the 6 million Quechua-speaking people are descendents of the Incas. The mention of Llikichiri, a scary villain or "boogie man," was found in some research, but his influence was vague and evasive. In this play, he is used as Corriy's motivator and a measure of her bravery.

The Incas lived in mountain farmlands or villages, one of which was Chinchero, beautiful "town of the rainbows," which is still inhabited and supports one of the oldest markets in Peru. Their agricultural mountain economy was strengthened by excellent irrigation systems and terraced farmlands. Their lives were further sustained by raising llamas and alpacas, which provided them with transportation of goods, wool for weaving, dung for fuel, food, and hides for clothing and sandals. Other foods included guinea pigs, poultry, and dogs as sources of protein and crops such as maize, beans, potatoes, and quinoa as staples.

Along the length of South America, incredible roads, rock tunnels, and hanging rope bridges were engineered, built to last, and meticulously maintained by the Incas. Because they did not have a written language and had not encountered the wheel, messages were relayed from one location to another by a chain of runners. These young men, chasqui, trained from an early age, had to be strong, surefooted, and swift as well as have excellent memories. If chasqui failed to remember messages word for word, they were severely punished. There are no records indicating how many chasqui were trained within each town along the roadway or that young women were ever chasqui. Conch shells were carried by chasqui and used to announce their arrival at the next station. Although no written language had been invented, a number system using a string and knot device, called a quipu, was used to keep accurate records and information.

PARTS

Narrator 1

Narrator 2

Awki (grandparent): grandmother to Anka, Corriy, and Nina Nina

Anka (eagle, falcon): 16-year-old brother to Corriy and Nina Nina

Corriy (to run): nicknamed "Corri," 12-year-old sister to Anka and Nina Nina

Achachi (old person): nicknamed "Achi"

Tata: father to Anka, Corriy, and Nina Nina

Mama: mother to Anka, Corriy, and Nina Nina

Nina Nina (firefly): 10-year-old sister to Anka and Corriy

Tiyo (uncle)

Tiya (aunt)

Alcaldi (mayor)

Juku (owl): 11-year-old son of Alcaldi

Kayra (frog): 11-year-old boy, friend of Nina Nina

FLUENCY INSTRUCTION

Have students discuss the ages of the characters to help them reflect the maturity level in their reading. When you read aloud the script for students, have them listen for the following:

- Readers may choose to hold a word longer to convey an emotion. For example, the reader who voices Juku may choose to hold *Ah* in the line **Juku:** *Ah, I think I'll go home* to convey his hesitancy to eat anything prepared by Nina Nina. Read the line twice: once with *Ah* drawn out, and once with it read briefly. Have students compare the effect.

- Your voice rises very steeply at the end of a question that is both an exclamation and a question such as the children's alarmed *What?!? Why?*

- Italic is used to show where a word should be stressed to add meaning to the sentence such as on the line **Nina Nina:** *I remembered to **grind** the corn this time.*

COMPREHENSION

After you read aloud the script, ask students these questions:

1. How did Anka break his leg?

2. What did Alcaldi mean when he said that he didn't want to put the town "in a bad light"?

3. How did the men in the town of Chinchero view women? Support your responses with evidence from the script.

4. Identify and tell about a woman that you know who has overcome prejudice and stereotyping to contribute positively to society.

5. In what ways do stereotyping and prejudice affect a community or society as a whole?

TOP OF THE WORLD

PARTS

Narrator 1
Narrator 2
Awki (grandparent): grandmother to Anka, Corriy, and Nina Nina
Anka (eagle, falcon): 16-year-old brother to Corriy and Nina Nina
Corriy (to run): nicknamed "Corri," 12-year-old sister to Anka and Nina Nina
Achachi (old person): nicknamed "Achi"
Tata: father to Anka, Corriy, and Nina Nina
Mama: mother to Anka, Corriy, and Nina Nina
Nina Nina (firefly): 10-year-old sister to Anka and Corriy
Tiyo (uncle)
Tiya (aunt)
Alcaldi (mayor)
Juku (owl): 11-year-old son of Alcaldi
Kayra (frog): 11-year-old boy, friend of Nina Nina

Narrator 1: On a plateau more than 13,000 feet above sea level lies Chinchero, which means "town of the rainbow" in the Quechua language.

Narrator 2: Beautiful Chinchero, where the weather blows fierce with high winds, rain, and snow. Beautiful Chinchero, where no rain falls sometimes.

Narrator 1: Beautiful Chinchero, where people see snow-topped mountains and deep blue sky while they work terraced farmlands and herd llamas and alpacas.

Awki: Wake up, Anka! Even though your leg is broken, do not think you can sleep away the day.

Anka: Dear Awki, chasqui need their legs to run from post to post on our highways. Since I fell off the highway and broke my leg, I cannot do my work.

Awki: Do not worry. I will find you work! If you could walk, I would send you out for llama dung for our fireplace.

Anka: Oh no! I was afraid of that!

Nina Nina: Anka, who will take your place and run the highway?

Anka: No one. Usually each town has two chasqui and one in training.

Kayra: Who are our other chasqui?

Anka: Achi is the only one, but he is too old to run. He needs to train someone.

Awki: It is not enough to be swift, strong, and well balanced to be a runner.

Anka: You must also have an excellent memory!

Kayra: Why an excellent memory?

Ancient Civilizations Reader's Theater © 2004 Creative Teaching Press

Awki: The runner must remember the exact message, word for word, line for line.

Kayra: Oh!! I couldn't do that.

Awki: If the runner cannot do that, the Inca chief will throw him off the mountain!

Kayra: [gulp] I think I would rather raise llamas.

Nina Nina: Kayra, you never run; you always hop and jump! But what if a message comes to our post and no one can run it to the next post?

Awki: Alcaldi could appoint someone in an emergency.

Anka: Let's hope that no message comes through.

Narrator 2: Awki takes her weaving out to the courtyard. Anka picks up the panpipes, but Awki shakes her head and nods toward the quipu.

Anka: I thought you might enjoy some panpipe music, Awki.

Awki: Later. Record information on the quipu before it leaves your head.

Anka: You know my memory is so good that I wouldn't forget.

Awki: What about the town's records if you had broken your neck, not your leg?

Anka: I was not in serious danger. I only slid down the mountain for 50 feet.

Corri and Juku: Hello! We've just come from the fields!

Juku: [breathless] You beat me again, Corri. You are not even out of breath.

Awki: Where is everyone else?

Corri: They are on their way. We ran across the terraces instead of the paths.

Awki: Juku, are you staying for breakfast?

Juku: What is for breakfast, Awki?

Nina Nina: I made some maize cakes.

Juku: Ah, I think I'll go home.

Nina Nina: I remembered to *grind* the corn this time. I think they're fine today.

Corri: How hard are they? Do they bounce?

Juku: I'll take a chance and stay to eat. Here are the others.

Nina Nina: Mama, I think the maize cakes are okay today. Awki made the quinoa.

Mama: Good girl! And Anka, I see you are adding information to the quipu.

Anka: As if Awki would let me sit around and play the panpipes.

Tata: [laughing] If she said "later," then she hasn't changed!

Everyone: [laughing] Later! Later! She asked you to pick up llama dung too!

Tiya: Here's breakfast. Eat up. We'll have lots of work to do today in the fields.

Corri: Do you want me to run over to Alcaldi's for the digging tools?

Tiyo: That would save us time. Your feet seem to fly over the fields and terraces.

Juku: Corri, my father showed me where the tools are. I'll show you.

Tata: Then you better leave now, Juku! You know how fast she runs!

Everyone (except Corri): She is swift and well balanced. She flies like the wind.

Corri: When I run, I think about Llikichiri!

All the Kids: What!?! Why?

Corri: You know how scary Llikichiri stories are! I pretend he is chasing me.

Juku: So he makes you run faster?

Corri: Right.

Nina Nina: I would shiver and shake.

Kayra: I would jump off the mountain.

Tiyo: Is that what happened to you, Anka, our flying eagle?

Anka: Very funny. The fog confused me. I couldn't see.

Mama: Enough. Today, we irrigate fields since we've had no rain for weeks.

Tata: Our potatoes are ready to harvest. Tiyo and I will work that terrace.

Tiya: I can check the corn fields on the lower terrace.

Awki: If Corri brings me a squash, I will make guinea pig bean stew for tonight.

Everyone: Delicious!

Ancient Civilizations Reader's Theater © 2004 Creative Teaching Press

Top of the World

Tata:	Anka, when you finish with the quipu, cut llama leather for new sandals.
Narrator 1:	Everyone returns to work after breakfast. Corri and Juku run to Juku's house for tools. Nina Nina helps Awki with the weaving. While Kayra helps Anka cut leather from the neck of the llama hide, the mayor arrives.
Alcaldi:	[upset] Awki, where is everyone? I need them.
Awki:	We are the only ones here. Everyone has returned to work.
Alcaldi:	There's a problem. Here's Achi. He'll explain.
Achi:	A runner is at the post house. A message must continue south to Cuzco. If we break the chain, Chinchero will be punished.
Anka:	If we send someone untrained and they do not repeat the message exactly, the runner will be punished. Either way is bad.
Awki:	We have lots of fast runners.
Anka:	But we don't have fast runners with excellent memories.
Alcaldi:	That's why Achi has not trained anyone yet.
Nina Nina:	I know someone whose feet have wings and who never forgets a word.
Achi:	Wonderful! . . . Ummm . . . How do you know someone and I don't?
Kayra:	I know who!
Achi:	Who? Tell me.
Nina Nina:	Here she comes now!
All the Men:	Corri? Oh no! No! No! Absolutely not!
Corri and Juku:	Hello, everyone!
Corri:	Here's the squash for tonight's meal, Awki.
Juku:	What's going on here? We could hear "No, no."
Narrator 2:	As Achi and Alcaldi explain the problem to Corri and Juku, Mama and Tiya quietly walk into the courtyard and listen.
All the Men:	So no, no! Corri cannot be sent.
Children:	Why?

Achi: You see, chasqui are boys or men.

Nina Nina: Why?

Anka: We are well balanced, brave, strong, and have excellent memories . . .

Nina Nina: Who has a broken leg because he fell off a highway in the fog?

Anka: Quiet! . . . and girls would be afraid.

Nina Nina: Corri wouldn't.

Juku: She *likes* to think Llikichiri is chasing her.

Kayra: That's enough to scare me, but not Corri.

Achi: Even if she were strong and brave enough, there are other problems.

Alcaldi: As mayor, I will not put our town into a bad light.

Mama: [a little angry] Our town in a bad light? Sending Corri puts our town in a good light because she can do the job perfectly!

Tiya: Because a girl can run and remember as well as a boy?

Mama: Be sensible, Achi.

Tiya: It's been two years since you retired and no new chasqui have been trained.

Mama: Face it! There is no one.

Tiya: Even if there were, Corri would still be the best.

Awki: She was born to run and run and run. And she does all day long.

Nina Nina: As for memory, she tells us the old Llikichiri stories word for word.

Kayra: When travelers visit, Corri listens to their stories and retells them to us.

Mama: When Tiya and I were girls, Awki encouraged us to use our talents to help our town and we did. We developed better ways of farming and raising llamas.

Tiya: We've invented the best watering system for our terraces. People come to us to learn because water during a drought keeps us alive.

Mama: We have bred the best llamas. They have the softest and warmest wool, the most tender llama meat, the heaviest hides, and . . .

Ancient Civilizations Reader's Theater © 2004 Creative Teaching Press

TOP OF THE WORLD

Anka: [laughing] And your llama dung is the easiest to pick up and store, too.

Awki: Corri, what do you think? Can you help the people of Chinchero?

Corri: Yes. I can run the course swiftly. My memory is good, too.

Achi: Even though the highways and bridges are smooth stone, they still climb up and down the mountains. It is a rough run.

Alcaldi: As mayor, chasqui report to me about rock slides, damaged highways, and bridges and rock walls that are in need of repair.

Corri: That's no problem. Who told you about the half-mile rock slide last year?

Alcaldi: Ummm. You.

Corri: Who told you about the bridge with bad damage from the ice?

Alcaldi: Ummm. You.

Corri: Who told you about the rock wall that was ready to fall?

Alcaldi: Ummm. You.

Achi: I think it is time to change our ways and give Corri a chance.

Everyone: Hooray!

Narrator 1: When Corri is ready to run, everyone gathers to cheer her on.

Alcaldi: Here is your conch shell, Corri, to announce your arrival at the next post.

Tata: I am proud that you will help our beautiful Chinchero and her people.

Tiyo: May Inti, our sun god, safely guide your feet along the path.

Corri: Thanks you all. I am off now.

Nina Nina: Don't let Llikichiri catch you!

RELATED LESSON

A History of Communication: Picture This!

OBJECTIVE

Research and learn more about the history and advancement of communication, illustrate the history of communication and advancements throughout the ages via a class mural, and share information with the class.

ACTIVITY

After reading the script, divide the class into small groups of three to four students. Have groups use the **Internet, reference books, and trade books** to research the history of communication by choosing one of the following areas: smoke signals, telegraph, printing press, telephone, pony express, postal service, radio, television, or e-mail. Once groups have completed their research, have them share the information with the entire class and sequence the communication events by creating a timeline on the board. Once all groups have shared and the timeline is complete, have students work cooperatively to visually depict the history of communication by creating a class mural. Have students plan their illustration and create a rough draft before transferring their work onto **large pieces of butcher paper** that can be pieced together sequentially to create the larger, complete mural. Have students think of a creative title for the mural, and display it in the classroom or hallway for others to enjoy.

THE MAYA

ANCIENT
CIVILIZATIONS

VOCABULARY

Discuss the meaning of each of the following words. Divide the class into pairs, and ask them to write a sentence using one of the words. Then, have pairs take turns reading their sentence to the class, *omitting* the vocabulary word. Have the rest of the class use the context of the sentence to identify the missing word.

ancestor: a person from whom one is descended; forefather

architect: a person who plans and supervises the construction of buildings

gourd: a plant related to the pumpkin, squash, and cucumber whose shell is sometimes used to make musical instruments and bowls

harmony: agreement in feeling or opinion

jade: a pale green or white mineral that is used in making jewelry

lyric: words to a song or poem

obsidian: a kind of black glass produced by volcanoes

Pok-a-Tok: a Mayan ball game played with two teams that was similar to soccer and basketball

BACKGROUND

Today in southern Mexico, the Yucatan Peninsula, Belize, and Guatemala, over 6 million Maya people still live in volcanic highlands and in lowlands that are part rain forest and part forest. Lost cities, mysterious writings, tombs, and treasures are part of Maya history that can be traced back to 1500 B.C. and prospered from A.D. 250 to A.D. 900.

In this play, the premise that the Maya tried to exist with nature in a harmonious relationship grew from a Maya proverb: "Who cuts the trees as he pleases, cuts short his own life." Even today, contemporary Maya live in harmony with neighbors according to this ancient rule.

The Maya excelled in several areas, such as architecture, agriculture, land and sea trading, engineering, and mathematics, including the use of zero. Their complex writing on stone, wood, and books (codices) was decoded in the mid-1970s, revealing much about them and their culture.

In this play, Mah Kina, My Ruler, is a fictitious composite of many rulers of the Maya civilization. A ruler would have worn much gold and silver jewelry, precious gems, a feather headdress, jaguar skins, and more. He, as well as others, would have been considered attractive with a hooked nose, slightly crossed eyes, a cone-shaped head, and teeth filed into points or a "T" and inlaid with precious stones.

Pok-a-Tok, or ulama, was more than a ball game. Professional ball players were coached by priests to win support of their gods. Presumably, the losers were sacrificed to pacify the gods. There's no basis that a band would have been allowed to perform before a Pok-a-Tok game, but the instruments mentioned are accurate and would have been available. References to specific foods are precise, including the reference to chewing gum, which was made from tree sap.

PARTS

Narrator 1

Narrator 2

Ix (jaguar): an inventive, mischievous 11-year-old son of the high priest and twin to Ik

Ik (wind): a creative, headstrong 11-year-old daughter of the high priest and twin to Ix

Kayab (turtle): a cautious, inquisitive 11-year-old boy

Kawak (storm cloud): a gloomy 8-year-old girl

Mah Kina (my ruler): the confident ruler of the Mayan city, father to Ix and Ik

Imix (waterlily): an outspoken 12-year-old girl

Men (eagle): an alert, keen 10-year-old boy

Yax Pac (rising sun): a knowledgeable, focused 12-year-old girl

Chob (red): an artistic, attentive 12-year-old boy

Maloob (fine): a cheerful 8-year-old boy

FLUENCY INSTRUCTION

Focus students' attention on the character descriptors provided. Ask them to relate each character to someone they may know who might be described in a similar way. When you read aloud the script for students, have them listen for the following:

- Kawak is described as gloomy. Read one of his lines, modeling a low pitch, slow pace, and occasionally melodramatic intonations.
- Mah Kina is a confident and demanding adult. Model reading his lines with an almost marching pace. His lines should always be read in a clear voice that carries. Mah Kina would not speak softly or swallow his lines.
- Maloob is a cheerful character. Model reading his lines with a quick pace and upbeat pitch.

COMPREHENSION

After you read aloud the script, ask students these questions:

1. Name at least three items that Mayan traders brought from other areas.

2. What did Ik mean when she said, "our goose will be cooked"?

3. Why did Ix and Ik suggest that the group be named The Roaring Jaguars?

4. How did the ancient Mayan people work together to create the Mayan culture?

5. Do you think that Imix was foolish or wise to question the high priest without getting his permission to do so? Give reasons to support your answer.

MAYA ROCK

Ancient Civilizations Reader's Theater © 2004 Creative Teaching Press

PARTS

Narrator 1
Narrator 2
Ix (jaguar): an inventive, mischievous
    11-year-old son of the high priest and
    twin to Ik
Ik (wind): a creative, headstrong
    11-year-old daughter of the high
    priest and twin to Ix
Kayab (turtle): a cautious, inquisitive
    11-year-old boy
Kawak (storm cloud): a gloomy 8-year-
    old girl
Mah Kina (my ruler): the confident ruler
    of the Mayan city, father to Ix and Ik
Imix (waterlily): an outspoken 12-year-
    old girl
Men (eagle): an alert, keen 10-year-old boy
Yax Pac (rising sun): a knowledgeable,
    focused 12-year-old girl
Chob (red): an artistic, attentive
    12-year-old boy
Maloob (fine): a cheerful 8-year-old boy

Narrator 1: A group of youngsters has gathered in the early evening in an outdoor courtyard surrounded by emerald green trees. The stone benches are still warm from the setting sun.

Ix: Ik and I have asked you all to come tonight to talk about forming a band.

Kayab: A band? What?!? I'm leaving! I can't be in a band of robbers!

Kawak: I don't think this is a good idea!

Ix: No! No! A band of musicians.

Ik: Yes, some musicians and some singers.

Kayab: What will these musicians and singers do?

Ix and Ik: Perform!

Kayab: Perform? Slow down, Ik and Ix! Where? Why?

Ix: Kayab, we know you are careful in making decisions, and that is why we need your help. Here comes our father to explain everything.

Narrator 2: Into the courtyard walks a sturdy man, the father of Ix and Ik, wearing much jewelry, a headdress decorated with feathers, and a jaguar skin cape. He is Mah Kina, the high priest and the ruler of the Maya city.

Narrator 1: When he smiles, his teeth, filed into sharp points and covered with pieces of jade and gold, shine in the last rays of the setting sun.

Mah Kina: You will form a band to perform at the opening Pok-a-Tok ball game. The game will be in two weeks. You must have the *right* kind of music. Now, since there are no questions, I am on my way.

Imix: Oh Mighty Mah Kina, I have a question.

Kawak: I don't think that's a good idea!

Mah Kina: Imix, *you?* No questions!

Imix: I know, but what kind of music is the right kind?

Mah Kina: The *right* kind of music is not the wrong kind, of course. You will know it when you hear it.

Narrator 1: The ruler leaves the courtyard.

Chob: There is something strange here.

Imix: We didn't ask to start a band, did we? Oh, Ix and Ik, what did you do?

Ik: Well . . .

Ix: We knew everyone wanted to start a band!

Everyone (except Ik and Ix): *We* did? Huh?

Yax Pac: Remember the last time Ix and Ik had a plan? Men, you have a great memory. Tell the story.

Men: Of course. The twins persuaded Chob to paint the Red House to honor the returning traders. Ix painted the welcome sign on it.

Chob: The painting was great; the welcome sign was not.

Yax Pac: Having Ix write the glyphs was a mistake.

Kawak: Oh-oh! A huge mistake!

Imix: Ix is not good at knowing which of the 800 glyphs to use, is he?

Men: Instead of writing "Thanks for bringing obsidian, pottery, fish, and sea shells," Ix's glyphs said "Thanks for bringing your black, fishy, smelly socks!"

Maloob: It's a good thing that Imix isn't shy about talking to Mah Kina to get us out of trouble.

Ancient Civilizations Reader's Theater © 2004 Creative Teaching Press

MAYA ROCK

Kayab: That was quick thinking on your part, Imix. We might have been thrown into the Sacred Pond and drowned!

Men: Our ancestors would have approved.

Kawak: But it would have been a very bad thing for us!

Kayab: Hmmmmm. We should have checked Ix's writing.

Ix: That's true, but that's enough about my mistakes.

Men: [laughing] What about Ik and her bright idea to turn tree sap into something to chew?

Chob: Our beautiful woven clothes, our hair, and our skin turned orange and brown.

Men: Remember how sticky we were? The ants and flying bugs couldn't fly off once they landed on us!

Kawak: Yuck! That was creepy!

Ik: Actually, I'm still working on that idea.

Everyone: Ohhhhhhh, please, no!!

Ik: I knew you'd be happy! I'm going to call it chewing gum! But let's get back to the band!

Maloob: Who has some ideas?

Chob: We will need costumes!

Yax Pac: Lots of feathers!

Ix: Leather bracelets!

Ik: And bright colors . . .

Yax Pac: Chob, will your father, the jewelry maker, give us some gold, silver, and jade?

Chob: Only if we have goods to trade. Now, I'll start planning the costumes right away!

Imix: Wait! Aren't you forgetting something?

Yax Pac and Chob: No, we don't think so.

Imix: We are not a band. We do not have any music or any words for a song.

Kawak: This is not going to work.

Ancient Civilizations Reader's Theater © 2004 Creative Teaching Press

Ik: The traders brought back some new instruments: clay whistles, shell rattles, and copper bells.

Maloob: With our musical background we'll be playing them in days!

Ix: We are already good at playing the gourd rattles, the drums, and the flutes. We do make great music.

Kayab: I think we can make the music with no problem.

Chob: True, we can, but this band will need lyrics, too.

Kayab: The *right* kind of music means the *right* kind of words. Let's do this correctly.

Ix: NO problem! I've made up words for a song. They are the best! Listen: [softly chant] Pok-a-Tok is a game we play. The ball is hard, made of rubber not clay.

Kawak: Oh, this is bad.

Everyone (except Ix): If that's your best, then we're in trouble.

Chob: Where are you going, Kayab?

Kayab: To jump into the Sacred Pond before Mah Kina throws us in.

Maloob: Wait! Does anyone else have words for a song?

Imix: I might. Listen: [softly chant] No questions asked, no answers gained. Ask one or two, it's all the same. It makes no difference who you are, just ask away. You'll go far.

Ik: I like it, but it's *your* song, Imix.

Yax Pac: It's right for *you,* Imix, because you ask lots of questions.

Men: Kayab, what do you think?

Kayab: Hmmm. Yes, it's not quite right for everyone.

Maloob: Any other ideas?

Yax Pac: How about a song about the helpful people in our city? Listen: [softly chant] The farmers keep us well supplied with tomatoes, squash, and beans on trays. On hot stones we can fry flat tortillas ground from maize.

Yax Pac: Yes! We can sing about the potters who make pots.

Ik: Don't forget the architects who plan and build our stone buildings.

MAYA ROCK

Chob: How about the people who make the jade, gold, and silver jewelry?

Imix: We can't forget the people who study the sky and make our calendar.

Kayab: The people who take care of the math, the counters, the . . .

Ix: Remember the writers of the codices, the people of the trees, and so many others.

Ik: There are too many important people! If we forget anyone, our goose will be cooked!

Kawak: This sounds bad. I'm glad I don't have a goose.

Men: Let's just say we won't be worried about any goose. Anyone not remembered in the song will throw us into the Sacred Pond!

All: Ohhhhhhhh!

Narrator 2: Unnoticed by the children, Mah Kina quietly returns to the shadows of the courtyard.

Maloob: I think we are getting closer to the right words, but something is still missing.

Narrator 1: The sky is darkening. The torches in the courtyard are lit. The children are quiet while trying to think of lyrics to a song.

Narrator 2: From the forest come the sounds of night activity. The mighty roar of a jaguar is followed by squeals from a wild pig caught by the powerful cat. The frogs and insects begin their night music.

Narrator 1: As the quetzals and other birds settle themselves into quiet, the owls give a wake-up call, stretch their wings, and softly flutter away to find their food.

Narrator 2: The rustle of leaves and bushes wakes up the lazy dogs that sneak off to look for snakes. Maloob snaps his fingers.

Maloob: I have an idea for a song.

Imix: What is it?

Maloob: What have you been feeling in the past few minutes?

Kawak: Tired and worried!

Maloob: Who felt afraid?

All (except Maloob): Not me! Why?

Maloob: That's it. We all feel fine! We are not afraid!

Ancient Civilizations Reader's Theater © 2004 Creative Teaching Press

Imix: How do we write a song about not being afraid?

Maloob: No, not that. We feel comfortable with everything around us—nature, the forest, our city, our world.

Men: Our families and ancestors have always felt that way.

Yax Pac: I see what you mean, Maloob. Write words that show how we live in harmony with our world.

Maloob: Exactly!

Ix: Amazing!

Kawak: But how do we know that's *right*?

Ik: I think Maloob is on the right track! Our ancestors lived in harmony with nature. Kayab, what are your thoughts?

Kayab: Hmmmm . . . I think if we write about harmony in our world, we will have the right kind of music.

Men: All of our people will feel the rightness of the words.

Maloob: Right on! Listen: [softly chant] In days of old our tales were told by ancestors who were wise. They knew how to plant, how to build, how to chant, to heal using flowers and dyes. Connected to the earth. Connected to the sky. They touch us today. They are with us—you and I.

Mah Kina: I have been watching and listening. You have the right music for the Pok-a-Tok.

Ix and Ik: We won't be thrown into the Sacred Pond?!

Mah Kina: No. At least, not *this time!*

Kawak: Whew!! But . . . there is still a problem!

All (except Kawak): What now?

Kawak: The new band needs a name!

Ix and Ik: Well, that's not hard: The Roaring Jaguars!

Ancient Civilizations Reader's Theater © 2004 Creative Teaching Press

RELATED LESSON

Maya Culture Quest

OBJECTIVE

Compare and contrast components of the ancient Maya culture to components of students' own cultural backgrounds.

ACTIVITY

After students read the script, have them tell what they learned about the ancient Maya culture, and record their responses on **chart paper.** Then, divide the class into small groups based on the categories on the **Maya Culture Quest reproducible (page 36).** Give students **trade books, textbooks, and other reference materials** to help them gather additional information. Once groups have completed their research, give each group a copy of the reproducible, and have groups compare and contrast their assigned area of the ancient Maya culture to their culture. Have groups share their findings with the whole class. You may have audience members use the information provided by each small group to complete the remaining sections of the chart.

Here are some useful Internet sites:
Mayan Culture, Oddities, and Games: www.halfmoon.org/culture.html
The Mayan Astronomy Page: www.michielb.nl/maya/astro.html
Maya Ruins: www.mayaruins.com/
Mayan Folktales: www.folkart.com/~latitude/folktale/folktale.htm
Mexico Connect, The Classic Period: www.mexconnect.com/mex_/hclassic3.html
Science Museum of Minnesota, Welcome to Maya Adventure: www.sci.mus.mn.us/sln/ma/
Maya Art and Books: www.maya-art-books.org/
Mayan Splendorous Culture: victorian.fortunecity.com/tiffany/467/mayancul.htm
The Pok-A-Tok Game: www.megalink.net/~jonb/webquest/games.html

These are some trade books students might find helpful:
Mayan and Aztec Mythology by Michael A. Schuman (Enslow Publishers)
Mayan Folktales: Folklore from Lake Atitlan, Guatemala by James D. Sexton
  (University of New Mexico Press)
Secrets in Stone: All About Maya Hieroglyphics by Laurie Coulter (Little, Brown and Company)
Step into the Aztec & Mayan Worlds by Fiona MacDonald (Lorenz Books)
Your Travel Guide to Ancient Mayan Civilization by Nancy Day (Runestone Press)

Maya Culture Quest

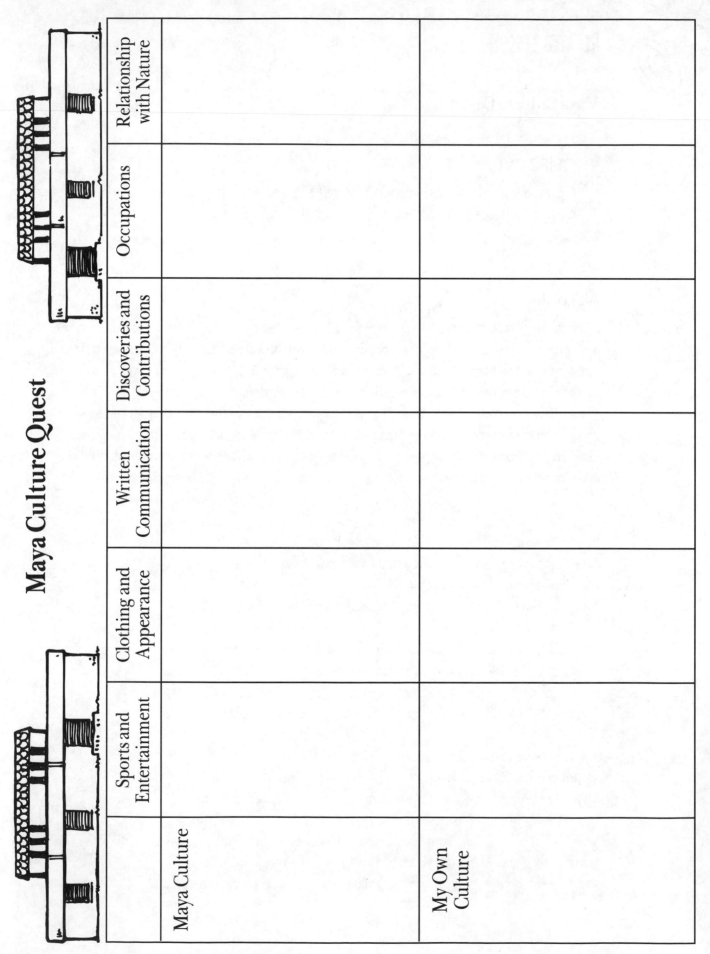

	Sports and Entertainment	Clothing and Appearance	Written Communication	Discoveries and Contributions	Occupations	Relationship with Nature
Maya Culture						
My Own Culture						

Ancient Civilizations Reader's Theater © 2004 Creative Teaching Press

THE ETRUSCANS

ANCIENT
CIVILIZATIONS

VOCABULARY

Discuss the meaning of each of the following vocabulary words. Then, choose a word, and draw lines to represent the number of letters it contains. Invite students to guess letters in the word. Record correct student responses until the word is identified. Have the student who identifies the complete word supply the remaining letters and define the word or use it correctly in a sentence.

artifact: an object produced or shaped by humans, such as a tool, weapon, or ornament, which is of archaeological or historical interest

excavate: to remove by digging or scooping out

forge: to form or shape metal by heating it in a furnace and beating or hammering it into shape

grant: money given for a specific purpose

gruel: a thin, watery porridge

plateau: an elevated, level piece of land

sarcophagi: stone coffins that were often inscribed or decorated with sculpture

BACKGROUND

From 900 B.C. to 90 B.C., the 20,000 Etruscans lived, worked, and influenced what was to be the great Roman Empire. Tarquinia, the location of this play, was a powerful city and cultural capital of Etruria. Today, discoveries about the Etruscans are found under paved streets and overgrown lands in abandoned tombs in northwestern Italy.

Archeologists have not decoded the Etruscan written language. Tomb translations, such as *Api*, which means *Father*, are limited. Imagine trying to understand a culture or to break a code only by reading tombstones.

The Etruscans were skilled workers of iron, bronze, and precious metals. They were engineers of bridges, roads, and sewer and drainage systems. They raised animals and grew grains, olives, and grapes. Their tombs indicate that they enjoyed sports, religious ceremonies, and feasts with music. They dressed in brightly colored robes, and some women, probably aristocrats, wore high-soled sandals with gold laces. Even though they wrote over 13,000 books, none survived.

The only sculptor's name that endures is Vulca, whose Apollo of Veio, can be seen in the Etruscan Museum of Villa Giulia in Rome. At the Etruscan Museum at Tarquinia, one statue is identified as Laris Pulena, son of Larce, nephew of Larth, and although the play includes the names Laris, Larce, and Larth, the development of them as characters in this play is fictitious.

Etruscan priests were called haruspices. They wore cone-shaped hats and examined sheep's livers as a way to predict the future. In the play, Haruspice and his predictions are imaginary. Perhaps if Haruspice truly knew that the Etruscan culture would be a mystery to future peoples, steps, such as a safe-storage room, would have been created and used by these mysterious people.

PARTS

Narrator 1

Narrator 2

Phillip Troth: 12-year-old son of Will and Janice Troth

Polly Troth: 11-year-old daughter of Will and Janice Troth

Heather "Hedy" Troth: 9-year-old daughter of Will and Janice Troth

Will Troth: father of Phillip, Polly, and Hedy

Janice Troth: mother of Phillip, Polly, and Hedy

Laris: son of Larce, nephew of Larth, a 12-year-old Etruscan boy

Larce: father of Laris, brother of Larth

Haruspice: an Etruscan priest who foretells the future using sheep's livers

Astrea (Etruscan goddess of justice): mother of Larce

Larth: uncle of Laris, brother of Larce

Jana (Etruscan goddess of the moon): 10-year-old Etruscan daughter of Haruspice

FLUENCY INSTRUCTION

Have students discuss the ages of the characters to help them reflect the maturity level in their reading. When you read aloud the script for students, have them listen for the following:

- Some lines need to be read by two people together. Point out that the line may be read by both people at exactly the same time, or very slightly overlapping (which sounds more natural), but if there is too much of a difference in the timing, the audience will not be able to understand the line. Have volunteers model reading **Will and Janice:** *That's great! Don't give up* together.

- Point out that a word in quotes such as in the line **Polly:** *We need "instructing" very, very much* may be easier for the audience to understand if there is a very slight pause before and after the word to set it off. Read the line and model the pause.

COMPREHENSION

After you read aloud the script, ask students these questions:

1. Why is Janice Troth sad about going home to Pittsburgh?

2. What is Janice and Will Troth's occupation? What cues in the script suggest this?

3. How would you describe the personality of each Troth child? Support your responses with evidence from the script.

4. How are present-day people able to learn about ancient civilizations and people?

5. Do you think the Etruscan civilization was important enough for the Troths to study further? Explain why or why not.

ETRUSCAN MYSTERY

Ancient Civilizations Reader's Theater © 2004 Creative Teaching Press

PARTS

Narrator 1

Narrator 2

Phillip Troth: 12-year-old son of Will and Janice Troth

Polly Troth: 11-year-old daughter of Will and Janice Troth

Heather "Hedy" Troth: 9-year-old daughter of Will and Janice Troth

Will Troth: father of Phillip, Polly, and Hedy

Janice Troth: mother of Phillip, Polly, and Hedy

Laris: son of Larce, nephew of Larth, a 12-year-old Etruscan boy

Larce: father of Laris, brother of Larth

Haruspice: an Etruscan priest who foretells the future using sheep's livers

Astrea (Etruscan goddess of justice): mother of Larce

Larth: uncle of Laris, brother of Larce

Jana (Etruscan goddess of the moon): 10-year-old Etruscan daughter of Haruspice

Narrator 1: At the end of summer 2004, in the Italian town of Tarquinia, northwest of Rome, the Troth family is excavating an ancient Etruscan site. They are eating lunch on a plateau overlooking the Tyrrhenian Sea.

Polly: You can almost feel the Etruscans living on this spot 2,000 years ago.

Will: I know. I feel the same way.

Janice: Yes, I sense that someone is looking over my shoulder, guiding my hand, saying, "Go, girl! Keep on digging! You'll find the secret of the code."

Phillip: The code?

Janice: Well, we know the Etruscan alphabet.

Will: And your mother has become quite good at reading their words.

Polly: But you have no idea what the words mean, right?

Janice: Right, Polly!

Will: None of the Etruscans' 13,000 books survived.

Hedy: But you know the words on the sarcophagi found in the tombs.

Will: Imagine understanding our culture by reading our grave sites.

Phillip: Yes. "Here lies John Smith, 1768–1849, loving father and husband."

Polly: Or "Jane Foe, 1899–1943. Rest in peace."

Hedy: I get it. There's not a lot about how we live on a tombstone.

Everyone (except Hedy): Right!

Janice: Sadly, we need to pack for our return trip to Pittsburgh.

Will: Our grant runs out this year so we won't return next summer.

Phillip: What!! But you have found so many new tombs!

Will: Sure, over 6,000 tombs have been found, but most of them are without decorations and artifacts, giving little information on Etruscan life.

Janice: We needed to find a unique tomb so that we could better understand the Etruscans or break their language code.

Polly: Do you need to find something important in order to renew your grant?

Will: Yes, and we haven't.

Hedy: I am not giving up. I am going to find something!

Will and Janice: That's great! Don't give up.

Janice: But we still go back in a few days.

Narrator 2:   Janice and Will Troth gather up the lunch bags and leave to make travel plans. Afternoon storm clouds cover the sky. Rain pours from the heavens. The children race to an earthen cave for protection.

Hedy: Look at the rock I found! It's so white and warm. I've named it Tages!

Phillip: Only you would name a rock! Why did you name it after Tages, a mystery boy who grew out of a plowed field?

Hedy: Tages was magical, and I know this rock is magical. Feel it.

Polly: It is warm! But, a magic rock? Ummmm.

Hedy: I'll make a wish and you'll see. Put your hands on Tages! [to the rock] Tages, help us to return to Tarquinia another summer.

Narrator 1:   Polly and Phillip are used to and amused by Hedy's games so they follow her direction. In a flash, they are in a cloud of hazy fog. Then . . .

Hedy: Wow! Look around. This isn't a cave anymore!

Ancient Civilizations Reader's Theater © 2004 Creative Teaching Press

ETRUSCAN MYSTERY

Phillip: Oh, my goodness, you've really done it this time, Hedy!

Polly: Yes, but *what* is it that she's done?

Narrator 2: The children are standing inside a house with three doorways. One door leads outside to a wet courtyard, one to a kitchen with cooking pots hanging in a corner, and another to a bedroom with several beds.

Narrator 1: From the courtyard comes the sound of people, music, and dancing. A boy, Laris, enters the room and the Troths freeze. Then an unusual reaction happens.

Laris: [to Phillip, Polly, and Hedy] Welcome! You made it! Come on!

Narrator 2: Laris runs back into the courtyard, leaving the three children with their mouths open, unable to react in any way.

Laris: They're here! Is everyone ready?

All the Townspeople (except Phillip, Polly, and Hedy): Yes! We're ready.

Narrator 1: The Troths walk carefully into the yard, which is filled with people.

Narrator 2: The people gathered are well dressed in brightly colored robes. The women wear high-soled sandals with gold laces.

All the Townspeople: Hurrah!! Hurrah! Let's get started!

Phillip (weakly): Please, explain. We don't understand.

Laris: [to the Troths] We wish you no harm. Api, they are frightened. Hurry.

Larce: Ahh-hem!! Welcome to Tarquinia! We are the Etruscans of Etruria. Our high priest will explain the "predicting."

Haruspice: Through the examination of a sheep's liver, I was able to predict that three visitors from another time would come today for a brief time.

Phillip, Polly, and Hedy: Us?

Larce: Yes. Now, my brother, Larth, will do the "instructing."

Polly: We need "instructing" very, very much.

Larth: According to Haruspice's foretelling, much about us Rasenna, as we call ourselves, will be destroyed. We want to live on in history. You can help.

Phillip: *Us?* We are only children.

Ancient Civilizations Reader's Theater © 2004 Creative Teaching Press

ETRUSCAN MYSTERY

Haruspice: [chuckling] Yes, but, children grow up. Continue, Larth.

Larth: We have planned a tour for you of our city of 20,000 inhabitants.

Larce: We have someone from each specialty to talk with you: skilled workers of bronze, iron, and precious metals; weapon and armor design people; bridge and road engineers; sewer and drainage engineers; and grape and olive growers . . .

Laris: Uncle Larth, our visitors could go to the port and talk with the sailors, too.

Larth: Thanks, Laris. Let's hope we have time.

Larce: Yes. Let's move on to the "seeing." Astrea, your turn with the children.

Astrea: We chose you because as you played on our land, you respected us.

Larth: We have guided your hands, turned your feet, and whispered into your ear.

Polly: We *do* feel guided. Mother speaks about that often.

Astrea: We hear her. We also hear her concerns.

Hedy: Who guided Tages to me?

Jana: I did! Tages is my magic rock. Now, we are connected through it.

Larth: In order to make the best use of our time, Astrea will take Polly, Laris and I will take Phillip, and Jana and Larce will take Hedy. We'll meet here at sundown.

Haruspice: Time is a concern. We cannot delay the children or all will be lost.

All the Townspeople: Hurrah! On with the tour!

Narrator 1: Phillip, Polly, and Hedy are led in separate directions with large crowds following. The tour is well planned with frequent stops at various shops and homes.

Narrator 2: Much later, the children reunite and talk about what they learned as everyone feasts on meats, vegetables, olives, olive oil, and gruel made from grains.

Hedy: I met Vulca whose sculpture, Apollo of Veio, survives and makes it to our day. I saw it last year.

Phillip: I saw how weapons and tools are forged at the ironworks.

Polly: They survive, but unfortunately, no written documents do.

Hedy: Mother knows your alphabet and figures out the words, but with no understanding.

Ancient Civilizations Reader's Theater © 2004 Creative Teaching Press

Etruscan Mystery

Astrea: Oh! We must correct that somehow.

Laris: Mother, time draws to a close. They must go back or . . .

Jana: What if they stay with us forever? Hedy and I could be best friends.

Hedy: Jana, if we stay, how could we make sure your history survives?

Haruspice: We have been given the gift of time with our visitors, but we cannot anger our gods by keeping them here.

Larce: We have one last sight for the Troths. Come quickly.

Narrator 1: The children are led back into the same room in which they arrived.

Larth: Walk 8 steps east, then 7 steps north. See the mud brick at Hedy's chin level. Push it into the wall.

Narrator 2: The wall swings back to reveal a secret room.

Polly: Oh! How beautiful.

Phillip: What is this, a tomb?

Jana: It's not a tomb of a person, but in a way it *is* a tomb.

Polly: What? A tomb, but not a tomb?

Laris: You've helped us to understand why so much of who we are is lost in history.

Jana: We prepared this bodiless "tomb" as a place to store our precious artifacts.

Laris: When you leave and for all of our future years, we will wrap and store our precious articles and books and store them in here.

Astrea: When you go back to your time, you'll have the location of this room.

Polly: Do you think we'll be able to find this exact place?

Larce: Our future depends on you.

Phillip: Then we will do our best.

Hedy: I won't give up! I will find this room!

Jana: Please keep Tages for me, Hedy. It belongs in your time now.

Hedy: Oh, it's warm again. Put your hands on it Phillip and Polly.

ETRUSCAN MYSTERY

Laris: Remember, you will feel us with you!

Narrator 1:   In a flash, they are in a hazy fog in the cave in which they had taken shelter in the afternoon storm. Now it is dark. Distant voices drift to the children's ears.

All: Phillip? Polly? Hedy? Where are you?

Phillip: Mother, we are here in this cave!

Janice: [breathless] You found a safe place! You're not even wet!

Will: The worst storm of the century and we couldn't get out here to find you! The weather station had no notice of the storm. It's as if it blew in from nowhere!

Polly: This storm was brewing for thousands of years!

Hedy: Oh, do we have a story for you!

Phillip: And maybe we'll be coming back next summer!

Narrator 2:   The children tell their parents the amazing story. And, of course, the parents think their children have made up a delightful tale.

Narrator 1:   With their final days in Tarquinia, Janice and Will decide to explore 8 steps east and 7 steps north in the cave just to satisfy the children.

Narrator 2:   Tages, safely tucked into Hedy's pocket, feels warm as the Troths break through the ancient wall into a bodiless "tomb" of Etruscan treasures. The Troth children whisper a silent "thank you" to the ancient people.

Ancient Civilizations Reader's Theater © 2004 Creative Teaching Press

RELATED LESSON

Shoe Box Time Capsules

OBJECTIVES

Create time capsules that include artifacts related to each student, his/her family and his/her culture and compose a letter explaining the significance of each artifact included in the time capsule.

ACTIVITY

Discuss with students the Etruscan culture described in the script. Then, tell students to imagine a time capsule that future civilizations will use to learn about today's people and culture. Explain that they will make shoe box time capsules. Give each student a **shoe box** and **art materials.** Ask students to decorate their box with illustrations that depict objects and ideas that represent present-day life. Have each student place these items into the time capsule:

- **an item that represents a personal achievement,** such as a certificate, ribbon, report card, or small trophy.
- **an item that represents the student's family.** This could include a family tree, a description and/or picture of a special family celebration, or a brochure from a recent family vacation.
- **an artifact that represents the student's culture.** A student might include an article of clothing or a magazine picture of current fashion, lyrics to a favorite song, artifacts to suggest current occupations, or a collage of food items.

Point out that the artifacts must fit inside the shoe box. Once students have decorated their time capsule and selected the items for inclusion, have them each write a letter to a person from the future who could eventually find and open the time capsule. Give students a **Letter to the Future reproducible (page 46)** to help them write the letter. Have students share their time capsule and letter in class before displaying them in the classroom or in the school's display case for others to enjoy.

Letter to the Future

Directions: Write a letter to an unknown person in the future. Your letter should contain five paragraphs as follows:

✔ **Paragraph #1—Introduction**

Use at least ten details about yourself, such as your name, date of birth, address, physical description, and personality traits.

✔ **Paragraph #2—Explanation of Personal Artifact**

Describe the personal artifact you chose and explain its significance.

✔ **Paragraph #3—Explanation of Family Artifact**

Describe the family artifact you chose and explain its significance.

✔ **Paragraph #4—Explanation of Cultural Artifact**

Describe the cultural artifact you chose and explain its significance.

✔ **Paragraph #5—Conclusion**

Conclude your letter by suggesting what you would like the recipient of the time capsule to do with its contents.

Ancient Civilizations Reader's Theater © 2004 Creative Teaching Press

VOCABULARY

Discuss each of the following words with students. Then, give each student a **Minoan Boat reproducible (page 58),** and have students use the appropriate vocabulary words to identify the parts of the ship.

apparition: a sudden or unusual appearance of a ghost

hold: the whole interior part of a ship below the lower deck, in which the cargo is stowed

hull: the main body of a large ship

keel: one of the main support beams (or plates) of a ship that can extend vertically into the water to keep the ship steady

seafaring: living life on or around the seas

stem: a curved piece of timber to which the two sides of a ship are joined at the front end of the ship

stern: the rear or back part of a ship

stowaway: a person who hides aboard a ship

sustain: to keep alive or to support something

BACKGROUND

From about 2200 B.C. to 1450 B.C. in the eastern Mediterranean Sea, the great Minoan civilization flourished on the island of Crete, 170 miles (275 km) long and 37 miles (60 km) at its widest. Although King Minos was a myth, Minos probably referred to a royal title given all rulers of Minoan culture.

The Minoans' wealth came from agriculture, architecture, engineering, arts, and seafaring and trading skills. In fact, because of their massive, powerful naval fleet, they were considered a thalassocracy, a government that dominated the seas.

In this play, a family sails to various Minoan sites to acquire items to trade. There is no evidence that families actually did this, but in the Minoan culture women had major roles in society and were free to travel and move about as they wished. Minoan traders sailed in single-sail boats with long upturned keels and bent-up prows to protect against dangerous storms and waves. At the port of Mochlos, seafaring traders would have collected the finest jewelry and hairpins to trade with Egypt, Cyprus, and other lands throughout the eastern Mediterranean Sea. At other ports, Vasiliki ware, the precursor to Kamares ware, would have been acquired. The use of the potter's wheel allowed artisans to make beautiful, delicate, thin pots and jars with handles and unusual pouring spouts.

The earliest writing of the Minoans on clay tablets was a combination of pictograms and hieroglyphs. Later, it evolved into writing that today is still undecipherable. As in this play, writing was essential to keep track of trading records. Finally, as in this play, when different peoples traveled, they influenced each other by forming friendships, appreciating differences, and exchanging ideas and knowledge.

PARTS

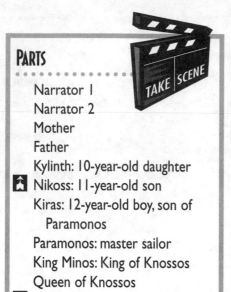

Narrator 1
Narrator 2
Mother
Father
Kylinth: 10-year-old daughter
Nikoss: 11-year-old son
Kiras: 12-year-old boy, son of
   Paramonos
Paramonos: master sailor
King Minos: King of Knossos
Queen of Knossos
Rissa

FLUENCY INSTRUCTION

Have students discuss the ages of the characters to help them reflect the maturity level in their reading. When you read aloud the script for students, have them listen for the following:

- Fluent readers naturally chunk, or group, smaller groups of related words together whenever they read longer sentences. Tell students that experienced readers oftentimes make very brief pauses within sentences whenever they are reading longer sentences such as in the line **Father:** *As we use our supplies, (pause for comma) we'll have more room for the goods (pause) we pick up along our route.*

- Commas provide a natural break in a sentence. Have students listen as you model a slight pause at the comma as in the line **Narrator 2:** *Because they live on an island, they depend upon the sea* and **Nikoss:** *I knew I'd need a warm jacket this morning, but I can't find it.*

After assigning parts for the script, encourage individual students to locate their lines and chunk them by inserting slash marks (/) at appropriate pausing points. Have students practice reading their lines with a partner.

COMPREHENSION

After you read aloud the script, ask students these questions:

1. Why was the family pleased to have Paramonos accompany them on their trip?

2. What did Father mean when he said, "This family has wandering blood"?

3. Why did Rissa take the items that she did?

4. Draw an illustration of the ship as you imagine it. Label the following parts: stem, stern, hull, keel, and hold.

5. If you could be a stowaway on a large ship, where would you like the ship to be going? Tell why.

TROUBLE ON BOARD

Ancient Civilizations Reader's Theater © 2004 Creative Teaching Press

PARTS

Narrator 1
Narrator 2
Mother
Father
Kylinth: 10-year-old daughter
Nikoss: 11-year-old son
Kiras: 12-year-old boy, son of
    Paramonos
Paramonos: master sailor
King Minos: King of Knossos
Queen of Knossos
Rissa

Narrator 1: On the island of Crete, in the eastern part of the Mediterranean Sea, lived an unusual seafaring family.

Narrator 2: Because they live on an island, they depend upon the sea. The entire family goes on trading trips throughout the Mediterranean waters.

Narrator 1: On this day in the year 1500 B.C., Father, Mother, Kylinth, and Nikoss are supervising the packing of their new, enormous boat with supplies to sustain them and to trade.

Mother: The items for trading should be packed in the stern hold. Our living supplies in the stem hold.

Father: As we use our supplies, we'll have more room for the goods we pick up along our trip.

Kylinth: Our sea route will take advantage of seasonal winds and currents.

Nikoss: With master sailor Paramonos with us again this trip, we'll be safe. He knows how to handle the boat when the thunder roars and the lightning flashes.

Mother: He's one of the few sailors who doesn't mind our whole family sailing. Kiras, how do you feel making your first sea voyage with your father?

Kiras: I've listened to his stories for years. Now I'll be part of the adventure!

Father: Because Paramonos has had so many experiences over all of the Mediterranean, he knows what to do in unusual emergencies, er . . . adventures.

Kylinth: Including the time that Nikoss was fishing and caught that enormous octopus. When it wrapped its tentacle around Nikoss' leg and tried to pull him overboard, Paramonos was right there and saved him.

Nikoss: Yes, weren't we all surprised!

TROUBLE ON BOARD

Paramonos: That octopus sure made for great eating for several nights!

Father, Mother, and Kylinth: A delicious meal!

Paramonos: We have had some great adventures, haven't we?

Kiras: I hope we have some this trip.

Mother: We will head east out of Knossos to make stops around Crete to pick up more goods for trading. Then, we'll trade with other islands and finally with Egypt.

Nikoss and Kiras: Hurrah!

Kylinth: We'll see Fadia and Farouk again!

Father: They'll be surprised to see us this year.

Kiras: Why? Who are they?

Father: Our Egyptian friends. Last year, I told them we'd see them in two years.

Kylinth: Why are we going this year, Father?

Father: The waters are much safer now that our navy patrols the sea.

Mother: Does having a new, swifter boat have anything to do with our trip?

Father: Yes it does. Our travel time will be cut in half.

Nikoss: And . . . we'd all rather be on the sea anyway.

Father: This family has wandering blood!

Mother: King Minos and the queen have requested us at the palace for a feast honoring our travels and new boat. Let's go!

Narrator: Later, in the Knossos Palace, the king sits on his new throne and talks with the family about their new boat and their travel plans.

Queen: Congratulations on your new boat!

King Minos: We depend upon your family to bring us new ideas and wealth from our neighbors. We know they look forward to our jewelry, pottery, and wine.

Queen: Will you have anything new to trade?

Ancient Civilizations Reader's Theater © 2004 Creative Teaching Press

TROUBLE ON BOARD

Father: Several of our Cretan artists have developed new seals to attach to doors or lids for containers. These seals act as locks.

Mother: The designs are most unique—made with the foreigners in mind.

Queen: Like what?

Mother: For the Egyptians, our artists have carved Egyptian birds and animals. For the medical people, a poisonous spider marks a seal for a dangerous potion.

King Minos: The information you bring back is as important for trade as the goods are! Keep up the good work.

Queen: We'll talk with you on your return.

Father and Mother: Thank you.

Narrator 2: The next morning is cold and dark as the seafaring family heads eastward in its fine new boat with the upturned keels.

Nikoss: I knew I'd need a warm jacket this morning, but I can't find it.

Mother: I saw you carry it onboard and put it on top of the dinner pots.

Kylinth: Maybe it fell. I'll go check for you. I'm sure it will turn up.

Narrator 1: The sunny day warms up as everyone works and enjoys the new boat. The cargo holds are well balanced. The boat is as swift and smooth as Father and Paramonos had hoped. Later, as the sun sets, Nikoss again looks for his jacket.

Nikoss: How strange that I haven't found my jacket.

Paramonos: Probably the sea goddess took it to keep warm.

Kylinth: You can't fool us, Paramonos; we won't fall for your tall tales anymore.

Paramonos: Ha! Ha! Ha! I remember the times when you would shake and tremble when I'd spin a hearty tale! No more?

Nikoss and Kylinth: We were just playing along with you, but no more!

Mother: I think we're all hungry. I brought a vegetable stew and enough bread for several days.

Nikoss: Let's eat!

Kylinth: Mother, how will two loaves of bread last us several days?

TROUBLE ON BOARD

Mother: What do you mean?

Kylinth: There are two loaves of bread in this pot.

Mother: I baked seven loaves this morning. Look again.

Paramonos: Now the sea goddess has claimed her share of the food.

Nikoss: This is very strange.

Kiras: With so much activity on board ship, maybe you forgot things.

Nikoss and Mother: We have not forgotten anything.

Mother: Let's eat what we have.

Narrator 2: It is a clear night on the waters. Everyone settles down for a good sleep. Paramonos and Father share the night watch. Suddenly, everyone wakes up.

Rissa: Ohhhhh! Ahhhhh! Ugghhhh!! Moan, moan, groan, eeeekkkkk!

Kylinth: What was that?

Kiras: Is that the sound of a new boat?

Father: Paramonos, are you teasing the children?

Paramonos: No, sir! It's stopped now.

Mother: Maybe it's the wind blowing through the air vents in the new hull?

Father: If we had air vents in the new hull, we'd be sinking!

Nikoss: There's nothing now. I'm tired. Let's go back to sleep.

Narrator 1: Everyone settles down again. As the sun comes up, the sailors wake up and begin another busy day. No one talks about the odd nighttime noises.

Kylinth: We should dock at Mochlos later today where we'll pick up some of their finest jewelry for trading.

Mother: We have room for jewelry and a few dark red Vasiliki vases.

Kylinth: Soloss was going to make me a hairpin with a flower head on it.

Kiras: Remember some extra bread!

Ancient Civilizations Reader's Theater © 2004 Creative Teaching Press

TROUBLE ON BOARD

Nikoss: Mother, Father wants the water jug. Do you have it?

Mother: No, Nikoss, tell him it hangs where it usually does.

Nikoss: I looked there first, but it's not there.

Mother and Kylinth: What? What is going on around here?

Nikoss: I really don't know, but something's fishy! Let's look around.

Narrator 2: After checking the boat from stem to stern, nothing seems unusual. Later, everyone goes ashore at Mochlos to see friends and to gather more trade goods. When they return to the boat, they sail around eastern Crete to the south toward Egypt.

Nikoss: Yes! We are finally on our way to Egypt. We can fish for our meal.

Kiras: No octopus please!

Kylinth: Wait until you see the wonderful goods the Egyptians have, Kiras.

Kiras: Are they very clever?

Nikoss: Very. I have been practicing their hieroglyphs so that I can read what they write about our trade goods. And I have become good with our writing so that my father will have all the trading information. Want to see?

Kiras: Sure! Maybe I could learn, too.

Nikoss: Ummm. That's odd. I just had my bag of clay tablets. Where's the bag?

Mother: Hi, kids, won't be too long before we're in Egypt! What's wrong?

Kiras: Nikoss can't find his bag of clay tablets. He just had them.

Paramonos: Sounds like the sea goddess is still playing jokes! I wonder why?

Narrator 1: Late that night, far from any land, the travelers sleep. Suddenly, they are awake again.

Rissa: Eeeeeiiiii! Ohhhhhhhhhh!! Ewwwwwww! Aaaiiiii!

Kiras: I don't think I like adventures on boats!

Nikoss: Is it the wind?

Father and Paramonos: There's no wind.

Mother: A sea monster! I've never seen one, but now we've heard one!

Ancient Civilizations Reader's Theater © 2004 Creative Teaching Press

Kylinth: It's gone now. We never heard anything like this on our old boat.

Rissa: Ewwwww. Uggggggh. Ohhhhh! Awwwwwwwww.

Father: Search the ship!

Kiras: That voice is a little bit familiar.

Paramonos: I'll light all the torches.

Mother: I think we'd better search the holds, too.

Narrator 2: The sailors search the ship from stem to stern, including the hold. Father steps out of the hold and pushes something ahead of him.

Father: Bring the torches! Look what I've found!

Everyone except Father: What?

Mother: A stowaway!

Nikoss: Exactly! And wearing my jacket!

Kylinth: And holding the water jug!

Father: What's left of the bread is down there. And I think a bag of clay tablets.

Paramonos: So it isn't a sea monster! Just a small stowaway with a loud scream.

Kiras: Father, I think . . .

Paramonos: Don't be frightened, Kiras, we know what to do with stowaways.

Father: Especially those who steal from us.

Nikoss: The sea law is quite clear and severe.

Rissa: Ohhhh!! Sob, sob, sob. Sniff, sniff, sniff.

Kiras: Father, bring the torch closer to the stowaway.

Paramonos: Sure, but why?

Kiras: Look!

Everyone (except Rissa): Oh, my goodness! How did you ever . . . ?

Rissa: I wanted to sail with you. These voyages sound like so much fun!

Ancient Civilizations Reader's Theater © 2004 Creative Teaching Press

TROUBLE ON BOARD

Kylinth:	Why did you scare us?
Rissa:	Every night I'd get seasick and I couldn't stop moaning and groaning.
Kiras:	It's my fault. My sister, Rissa, told me that she wanted to come with us.
Rissa:	No one would listen or take me seriously.
Mother:	Actually, we'll all take you seriously from now on!
Father:	What a relief! Welcome aboard, Rissa! You'll earn your keep now.
Rissa:	Great! I was so bored I borrowed Nikoss' clay tablets to learn to read!
Paramonos:	We'll be telling this story for years and years!

Ancient Civilizations Reader's Theater © 2004 Creative Teaching Press

RELATED LESSONS

Creating a Minoan Game

OBJECTIVES

Research aspects of Minoan life, create a card or board game that incorporates facts about Minoan life, write directions for playing the game, and devise an answer key for the game, if needed.

ACTIVITY

After students read and discuss the script, divide the class into pairs. Have partners use **reference books, the Internet, and trade books** to research one of the following aspects of Minoan life: trade, pottery, sports, food, achievements, occupations, legends, religion, music, fashion and clothing, art, and geography. After students locate related information, have pairs share the information with the entire class. Have students in the audience take notes from these presentations. Once all the pairs have shared, join pairs of students into small groups of four to six. Ask them to create a Minoan card or board game based upon the information learned from all of the student presentations. Have each group complete the following steps:

- Create a card or board game that incorporates information about the Minoan culture. (Encourage students to refer to their notes from the presentations.)
- Plan and make all needed materials to play the game. (Supply students with **poster board, construction paper, markers, scissors, glue,** and **other assorted art supplies.**)
- Write clear, concise directions for playing the game.
- Make an answer key, if needed.
- Invent a creative name for the game.
- Demonstrate how to play the game to the entire class. Have presenters share their written directions with the class and answer any questions they may have.

Invite groups of students to play the completed games. Students may need to revise their game directions after other students play their game and questions arise. Store the games in the classroom for continued student use.

Minoan Pottery: Vasiliki Ware Reproductions

OBJECTIVES

Research and learn about Minoan pottery and create and design a vase fashioned after Vasiliki ware.

ACTIVITY

Discuss with students how the Minoan people created pottery from clay. Pottery was first made by hand and later with the help of the potter's wheel. One type of pottery was known as Vasiliki ware, named after a Minoan village. This type of pottery was typically reddish-brown and decorated in a variety of colors, including red, orange, yellow, and white. The reddish-brown paint was applied over the entire surface of the vase. Minoan potters held burning twigs against the vase while it was still hot from the firing process to produce a mottled effect. Colorful scenes of Minoan life were then drawn or painted onto the vase.

Have students create their own Vasiliki ware by forming **self-hardening clay** into the shape of small vases. Once the clay dries and hardens, have students **sponge-paint** the exterior of the vase with **red and brown paint** to simulate the mottled effect. Give each student one each of the **Vasiliki Vase reproducibles (pages 59–60)**. Have students examine and discuss the samples and then draw original designs on the paper draft. Then, have them draw scenes with a **fine line black marker** and **paint** to complete the design on their clay vase. Finally, have students create an informational place card for their vase and share their pottery with the rest of the class. Place the vases and place cards in a showcase display.

Date _____

Minoan Boat

Directions: Label the *hold, hull, keel, stem,* and *stern* of the boat.

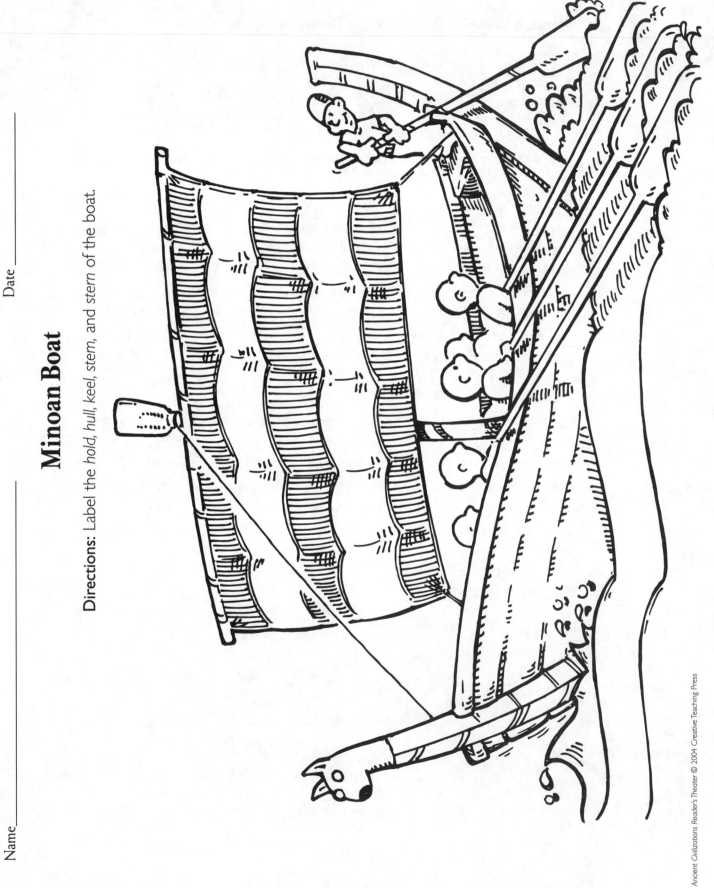

Vasiliki Samples

Directions: Use this page to get an idea of what an ancient Minoan vase looked like.

Name_____   Date _____

Vasiliki Vase

Directions: Use this page to plan the painting of your vase.

THE ROMANS

ANCIENT
CIVILIZATIONS

VOCABULARY

Discuss each of the following words with students. Then, have students identify the word they least understand. Have students research this word and then draw an illustration that clarifies the definition.

aqueduct: a long pipe used to carry water from a faraway source, usually by gravity

candidates: people who want to be or are nominated for an office, prize, or honor

contaminated: dirty or polluted

dredge: slang term for a dull or boring person

feats: courageous acts or deeds

gouger: a person who takes things away from others by using sly and dishonest ways

latrines: public toilets

plague: a widespread disease that is highly contagious

togas: loose-fitting, one-piece outer robes worn in public by male citizens in ancient Rome

treacherous: not able to be relied on; not dependable or trustworthy

BACKGROUND

The Roman Empire was the major power along the Mediterranean Rim from the 8th century B.C. to the 5th century A.D. Today, the area once occupied by the Romans is home to 40 different nations.

Many of the political characters in this play were citizens of the Roman Empire, but they did not all live at the same time. Julius Caesar and Mark Antony were acquainted with each other and probably with Marcus Licinius Crassus, whom the character Crassus in the play is loosely based upon. In fact, wealthy Crassus owned a private fire service that went to fires and demanded up-front payment from the property owner for the use of the fire services. Usually, he would acquire the fire-damaged property and rent the property back to the previous owner. He paid for a multiday banquet for 10,000 Romans. He sought political power through money. Because he wanted military glory as well, he bought his own army. Julius Caesar sent him and his army to Syria where he died in battle.

Augustus was a brilliant ruler who called himself "First Citizen" because of the Romans' hostility toward the title "king." His improvements included roads, bridges, aqueducts, walls, temples, tax reforms, census taking, and a tolerance for cultural diversity. The Roman political system would be recognizable to those familiar with modern democracy: more than one party, critics, fat-cat contributions, negative advertising, billboards, banners, and the right of citizens to gather, ask questions, and vote. The Forum was an open courtyard where townspeople gathered to discuss the running of the city and to listen to speeches.

Bringing Crassus and Augustus together for a Candidates' Crossfire was impossible as Crassus died before Augustus was born. The questions, answers, and political overtones are fictional.

PARTS

- Anna: reporter for the *Roaming Roman Rag*
- James: reporter for the *Roaming Roman Rag*
- Julius Caesar's Ghost
- Consul: former ruler of the Roman Empire
- Consul's Wife
- Marc Antony: leader of the Roman army
- Crassus: a candidate for Roman King
- Audience
- Augustus: a candidate for Roman King
- Doctor Daria
- Flavius: homeowner
- Nero: future ruler of the Roman Empire
- Livia: wife of Augustus
- Plautus: playwright
- Lili Lamplighter: maker and seller of lamps

FLUENCY INSTRUCTION

This script contains many alliterative phrases. Students should have fun with these, but they still need to be read in a way that retains the meaning. When you read aloud the script for students, have them listen for the following:

- Crude Crassus can collect countless chunks of coins from citizens.
- Finally, a fine faithful fellow and feat! First Citizen, fabulous!
- Doctor Daria dreads dirty diseases and disinfects dull dredges like you.
- Presto! The pace picks up and the politicians are pale.
- Attention! All actors, architects, artists, and adults applaud for Augustus' awesome ability.
- If this great greedy gouger governs our gates, we'll be grumpy and groaning. We'll get gruel and he'll get grade A steak!
- We watch, whisper, and wonder who will win. Weak or wise? Wait and see.

Have students practice their enunciation of words by reading and rereading the tongue twisters from the script with a partner. Stress to students that they must clearly pronounce each word in the tongue twister while saying it rapidly. Then, have students discuss the meaning of each phrase. Point out that the phrases work the best when the *meaning* is emphasized over the repeating phonemic element.

COMPREHENSION

After you read aloud the script, ask students these questions:

1. What event has caused the Roman townspeople to gather at the Forum?
2. What problems do the Roman citizens want the candidates to address within their city?
3. How are modern-day campaign issues similar to and different from the concerns of the ancient Roman citizens?
4. What qualities do you think make a good candidate for public office? Explain and justify your responses.
5. How do you think Candidates' Crossfire will end? Tell why.

CANDIDATES' CROSSFIRE

PARTS

Anna: reporter for the
    Roaming Roman Rag
James: reporter for the *Roaming Roman Rag*
Julius Caesar's Ghost
Consul: former ruler of the Roman Empire
Consul's Wife
Marc Antony: leader of the Roman army
Crassus: a candidate for Roman King
Audience
Augustus: a candidate for Roman King
Doctor Daria
Flavius: homeowner
Nero: future ruler of the Roman Empire
Livia: wife of Augustus
Plautus: playwright
Lili Lamplighter: maker and seller of lamps

Anna: The *Roaming Roman Rag* welcomes you to the Forum, the center of this great Roman city. We are glad to see so many townspeople gathered in this open courtyard for today's Candidates' Crossfire.

James: In a few moments, the questions and answers between the candidates for King of the Roman Empire will begin.

Anna: The rostrum is decorated with purple cloth, the color of royalty. People are dressed in their finest wool or linen togas.

Julius Caesar's Ghost: Purple is an expensive, kingly color. One of my favorites!

James: As your announcers, we'll interview some of the better known people here. Oh, here comes someone . . .

Anna: Excuse me, Consul. How do you think things will go today?

Consul: Not well.

Anna: What?? Why not?

Consul: I was not asked to run for king. I was overlooked.

Consul's Wife: And now I won't be First Wife of Rome! How sad!

Julius Caesar's Ghost: Whew! Maybe the Roman Empire will be safe! Marc Antony, what are you doing here? I thought you'd be in Egypt.

Marc Antony: You're looking a little pale, Julius. I thought I would scope out this scene in case I decide to be king someday. I do love Egypt though.

James: Attention please! Each candidate has twenty seconds for opening remarks before questions. Crassus, you're first.

Ancient Civilizations Reader's Theater © 2004 Creative Teaching Press

CANDIDATES' CROSSFIRE

Crassus: I am the best. I own so many things, like slaves, a fire department, silver mines, and more property in Rome than anyone. I paid for Julius Caesar's election and he was one of *my*—oops—I mean *our* best rulers! One thing I don't have is military glory . . . ummmm, I wonder . . .

Marc Antony: Military glory? Well, he is fit to clean the army's latrines!

Anna: Your time is up, Crassus, thanks.

Audience: Crude Crassus can collect countless chunks of coins from citizens. Choose Crassus!

Anna: Twenty seconds, Augustus.

Augustus: Julius Caesar was my great uncle. He was his own man and not owned or bought by anyone. Furthermore, I do not want to be your king.

Audience: Ewww? Not king? What? Why?

Crassus: Great! No elections. I'll be king!

Consul: Just a minute. I should be appointed.

Augustus: Fellow citizens, I want to work for and with you to build a great empire. I ask that you elect me "First Citizen."

Audience: Finally, a fine faithful fellow and feat! First Citizen, fabulous!

Julius Caesar's Ghost: Crassus never paid for my election!

James: Now for the first question. Remember the rules: You each will have thirteen seconds to respond. Augustus first.

Doctor Daria: What plans do you have for health issues? The plague will come again. Will we be prepared?

Augustus: Doctor, is contaminated water a problem?

Doctor Daria: Yes, many diseases are caused by water that is contaminated by wastes.

Augustus: I plan to build aqueducts to carry clean water into cities and a water system to take waste away through sewer lines.

Crassus: Without disease, our cities and empire will grow too big.

Audience: Doctor Daria dreads dirty diseases and disinfects dull dredges like you. Be careful, Crassus.

Ancient Civilizations Reader's Theater © 2004 Creative Teaching Press

CANDIDATES' CROSSFIRE

Marc Antony: As the army grows, we need clean water for the health of the army and those we conquer.

James: The next question, Crassus.

Flavius: You rushed to my house with your fire department when my house was burning down . . .

Crassus: Oh, yes, I remember.

Flavius: But you wouldn't put out the fire until I paid you.

Crassus: Correcto.

Flavius: I couldn't pay because my money was in my house. My house burned down. My question is: Do you see anything wrong with this?

Crassus: Zero. I bought your land after, didn't I? How good is that?

Flavius: Not good enough. Augustus?

Augustus: The idea of a fire department is a good one. We need to make sure all property is protected . . . from fire and thieves.

Nero: Let the fire burn. I will just play my fiddle! Then there will be nothing to worry about. No buildings, no taxes, no troubles . . .

Livia: No king!

Nero: Oh, what would I do with my future?

Livia: Fiddle for your dinner? Or start a fire insurance company?

Audience: Presto! The pace picks up and the politicians are pale. The powerful press will print plenty to read at a penny a page.

Anna: Plautus, whose new play, *E Tu, Brute?*, which means *And You Too, Brutus?*, has a question.

Julius Caesar's Ghost: I saw the play. All that dancing and singing while I'm dying on stage. That's not the way it happened! And those were not my last words. I said, "But I have a party tonight!"

Plautus: Candidates, would you protect the right of free speech?

CANDIDATES' CROSSFIRE

Crassus: I would—except for actors because they are the dredges of society. When I went to the play *Rockin' Romans,* I forbid my wife to sit in the first row in case the actors wanted to steal her.

Plautus: My actors are more careful than that, but I do understand why your wife might want to run away.

Augustus: Plautus, your plays have great story lines: runaway slaves, trouble in the streets, silly politicians, and foolish old men. If elected "First Citizen," I will protect the citizens' rights to speak, to gather, and to worship.

Audience: Attention! All actors, architects, artists, and adults applaud for Augustus' awesome ability.

James: One last question before closing words from the candidates.

Lili Lamplighter: Each time I enter the city to sell my lamps, I am taxed at the gate. I need my lamp money for my ten children. What will you do about taxes?

Crassus: Not everyone is as rich as I am. You could sell more lamps.

Augustus: Tax cuts for large families would help. A census or count of all the people in the empire would help us to know how much money—taxes—we need for our empire. Citizens shouldn't be overtaxed.

Crassus: What? I must have taxes to build my family a big palace.

Audience: If this great greedy gouger governs our gates, we'll be grumpy and groaning. We'll get gruel and he'll get grade A steak!

Anna: Remember, everyone is invited to a meal after this meeting. Tables are full of fish in an herb sauce, celery, breads, olives, olive oil, even steaks and roasts. Now to you, James.

Crassus: Ahem, I bought all the food. Thank you very much!

James: Candidates, in your closing tell how you will care for the empire, which includes 3,000 miles around the Mediterranean Rim and millions of different people and customs. You each have 15 seconds.

Crassus: Vote for me for King of the World! I have the most and am the best. I look great in purple. I will put your money to work. Trust me!

Ancient Civilizations Reader's Theater © 2004 Creative Teaching Press

CANDIDATES' CROSSFIRE

Augustus: All defeated people may become Romans and enjoy the benefits, water systems, new roads, and fair laws. Different people make us stronger, more interesting, and more considerate of each other.

Marc Antony: Earlier Crassus wanted military glory. Let's send him to Syria to fight the treacherous soldiers there. Let Augustus rule!

Audience: Hooray! Let Augustus rule!

Anna: I'm on my way over to the rostrum to hear from Crassus. Crassus, who won Candidates' Crossfire?

Crassus: No contest. I did!

James: I'm here with Augustus. Who won?

Augustus: The Roman people will be the winners on Election Day!

Doctor Daria: He has my vote.

Flavius: Mine, too.

Lili Lamplighter: I think he's honest. I hope his plans work.

Consul: I wonder if he could find me a job.

Consul's Wife: If not, we could cast doubt on the election.

Livia: Don't try. Election results are so respected that you'd look foolish.

Marc Antony: I'm off to Egypt where I'll live until I'm made king.

Julius Caesar's Ghost: Don't hold your breath. Augustus will be a great leader.

James: One last word from Livia.

Livia: Use your freedom on Election Day! Don't miss the boat. Vote!

Anna: Thanks to all who came. That's it for the *Roaming Roman Rag*.

Audience: We watch, whisper, and wonder who will win. Weak or wise? Wait and see.

Ancient Civilizations Reader's Theater © 2004 Creative Teaching Press

RELATED LESSONS

Candidates' Crossfire: Before and After Reading Guide

OBJECTIVES

Activate background knowledge, assess prior knowledge of the ancient Roman civilization, and provide a purpose for reading.

ACTIVITY

Before the class reads the script, give each student a **Candidates' Crossfire Before and After Reading Guide (page 69).** Ask students to answer the ten questions based on what they already know about ancient Roman civilization. Have them record their answers in the "Before" column. Before the class reads the script, tell students to listen for the answers to the questions as they read. After they finish reading the script, have them answer the same ten questions and record their answers in the "After" column.

A Picture's Worth a Thousand Words: Political Cartoons

OBJECTIVES

Examine the humor and commentary of political cartoons, draw a cartoon that depicts a situation from Candidates' Crossfire, and write an appropriate caption for a political cartoon using information from the script.

ACTIVITY

Share with students several examples of **political cartoons** from newspapers, and discuss them with the class. Ask *What makes the cartoon humorous? What serious message does the cartoon convey to the reader?* Give each student a **large piece of drawing paper,** and invite students to draw their own political cartoon based on the script. Have students include at least one of the candidates, depict at least one of the many concerns expressed by the Roman townspeople, and write a caption. Then, have them use the space below the cartoon to explain what the cartoon and how it relates to the caption. Invite them to share their cartoon with the rest of the class, and have the class discuss the issues in each cartoon. Encourage students to discuss whether the issues expressed in the cartoons are still issues in today's society.

Name_____ Date _____

Candidates' Crossfire
Before and After Reading Guide

Directions: Read each statement below. Write *true* or *false* in the first column before you read the script. After reading the script, answer each question again by marking your answers in the last column. Use the script to help you check your previous answers. Compare your responses before and after reading.

Before		After
	1. The meeting place at the center of Rome where people met to discuss issues was known as the Forum.	
	2. Navy blue was considered a color of royalty.	
	3. Romans wore wool and linen robes that were known as tobans.	
	4. Julius Caesar was Augustus' great uncle.	
	5. Water pollution was not a problem during ancient Roman times.	
	6. Plautus was a well-known Roman playwright.	
	7. The Roman Empire was small and consisted of fewer than one million people.	
	8. The Romans had no army and no way of protecting themselves from enemies.	
	9. Roman citizens were required to pay taxes.	
	10. The Roman people all shared the same customs.	

THE Chinese Han

ANCIENT CIVILIZATIONS

VOCABULARY

Discuss each of the following words with students. Then, have students choose one word to define and illustrate.

architect: a person who plans and supervises the construction of buildings

caravan: a large covered vehicle; van

famine: a severe food shortage that affects a wide area

govern: to direct or influence the behavior of others

ling: a Chinese ruler of a region or portion of the country

proverb: an old saying that expresses a truth about life

BACKGROUND

This play takes place in Chang-an, chosen by many emperors, including young Han Wu Ti, as the capital city of China. Actually, there were two Han dynasties: the original one from 207 B.C. to A.D. 220, which is used as the time frame for this play, and a later Han dynasty when descendents of the original Han dynasty regained control of China.

Education was important to Emperor Han Wu Ti (or Wu Di) who founded the Imperial University and a public school system for boys. Girls were allowed to learn calligraphy, poetry, and painting. In this play, an imaginary opportunity for the young women of ancient China is presented by suggesting Wu Ti was so advanced in his thinking that he would reward women who aided the empire by considering government positions for them. In fact, Wu Ti's reign was marked by the development of a central government, new agricultural practices, plans to prevent food shortages, innovative inventions such as an earthquake locator and paper, and the building of the Silk Road, connecting China and lands west for the purpose of trade.

Regional government workers, called *lings,* had a variety of duties to perform for the emperor. They had to impose order and laws, list individuals and property, collect taxes, arrange labor for public works, oversee schools, judge civil and criminal cases, and develop a variety of plans, such as the storing of grain in case of an empire emergency. Anyone who held public office had to take a civil service exam. At the time of Wu Ti's reign, about 135,285 officials held public office.

Ancient China is rich in proverbs from Buddhism, Taoism, and Confucianism. This play features numerous sayings that are meant to inspire people to think about themselves and to reach for goals despite preconceived ideas.

PARTS

Narrator 1
Narrator 2
Chen Long (dragon): the father of
   Shing and Hui Ying
Proverb Speakers
Chen Lei (chen lay) (flower bud): the
   mother of Shing and Hui Ying
Hui Ying (hoo-we ying) (intelligent):
   12-year-old girl, sister to Shing
Shing (victory): 11-year old-boy,
   brother to Hui Ying
Jian (jee-ahn) (determined):
   11-year-old girl
Mengnu (meng-noo) (fierce woman):
   10-year-old girl
An (ahn) (peace): 10-year-old boy
Ho (good): 10-year-old boy
Lok (happy): 12-year-old boy
Shen (deep thinker): 12-year-old boy
Man
Woman
Emperor Han Wu Ti or Wu Di
   (hahn woo tee or woo dee):
   16-year-old boy

FLUENCY INSTRUCTION

Have students discuss the ages of the characters to help them reflect the maturity level in their reading. When you read aloud the script for students, have them listen for the following:

- The pace of the reading speeds up when a character is excited. Have students name at least three places where the reading pace will pick up in this script.

- The Proverb Speakers read in unison. Point out that this means listening carefully while reading aloud so that your pace matches the pace of the other readers. Have a few different sets of volunteers model reading one of the proverbs. Invite students to notice that it works best when the readers also use the same intonation and volume as well as pace.

- The thieves are anxious and quick to be angry with each other. Point out that they will probably reflect this by speaking their lines sharply and quickly.

COMPREHENSION

After you read aloud the script, ask students these questions:

1. Where does the story take place?

2. How do the subjects that the Chinese boys are required to take in school differ from those the girls are required to take?

3. What are the responsibilities of a *ling*? What modern-day public official is most like a *ling*?

4. Chen Long told the children that they were "good citizens" when they reported the robbery plan to him. Do you think the children were good citizens? Tell why. How can you be a good citizen in your hometown?

5. If you had been one of the children, what would you have asked Emperor Han Wu Ti for as your reward? Explain.

SAVING THE SILK

PARTS

Narrator 1
Narrator 2
Chen Long (dragon): the father of
 Shing and Hui Ying
Proverb Speakers
Chen Lei (chen lay) (flower bud): the
 mother of Shing and Hui Ying
Hui Ying (hoo-we ying) (intelligent):
 12-year-old girl, sister to Shing
Shing (victory): 11-year old-boy,
 brother to Hui Ying
Jian (jee-ahn) (determined): 11-year-old girl
Mengnu (meng-noo) (fierce woman):
 10-year-old girl
An (ahn) (peace): 10-year-old boy
Ho (good): 10-year-old boy
Lok (happy): 12-year-old boy
Shen (deep thinker): 12-year-old boy
Man
Woman
Emperor Han Wu Ti or Wu Di (hahn woo
 tee or woo dee): 16-year-old boy

Narrator 1: In the capital city of Chang-an, Chen Long, the *ling* of a most respected region, prepares for a visit from Emperor Wu Ti.

Narrator 2: Chen Long's children and friends are ready to walk to school. The boys have lessons in reading, writing, history, and math. The girls have lessons in music, calligraphy, poetry, and painting.

Chen Long: Do your best at school today. Remember . . .

Proverb Speakers: "A closed mind is like a closed book, just a block of wood."

Chen Lei: After you return from school, the Emperor will visit. Now, go along so you won't be late.

Shing and Hui Ying: Good-bye!

Jian: I wish girls and boys could go to the same school. I want to be an architect and I need the math classes.

Mengnu: How will I become a warrior without history classes to teach me about the empire and the Emperor?

An: Impossible! Unless you cut your hair and dress as a boy.

Mengnu: Ummm. I'll think about it.

Shing: I want to be like Father. A *ling* is a most helpful person!

Ho: My parents say that your father is a kind and honest *ling*. They say . . .

Proverb Speakers: "Govern a family as you would cook a small fish—very gently."

Shing: Our father governs gently, with honesty and kindness.

SAVING THE SILK

Ho: What exactly does a *ling* do?

Lok: I bet he keeps everyone happy.

Shing: Father is happy when he does his best job to help others.

Mengnu: Is it his best job not to have equal opportunities for girls?

Hui Ying: Father does run the schools, but the Emperor makes the rules.

Ho: I'd like to help make good laws that people obey.

An: That's very interesting. I'm sure you would be a great lawmaker.

Proverb Speakers: "What you are now is what you have been; what you will be is what you do now."

Jian: Maybe I will work for a *ling* if there's a job that interests me.

Hui Ying: Father oversees the making of bridges, roads, and water canals.

Jian: I would love to build bridges!

Shing: The construction of the Silk Road is an enormous project that will take years. Many bridges are built over rivers and valleys.

Mengnu: I've heard of the Silk Road, but what is it exactly?

Ho: It's a trading road that connects our country with other countries.

Mengnu: What do we trade?

Hui Ying: We trade spices, rice, jewelry, and especially our beautiful, colorful, and costly silk. We send silk and bring back things we need.

Jian: I would like building bridges, as well as traveling the Silk Road.

Proverb Speakers: "Choose a job you love, and you will never have to work a day in your life."

An: I like being a judge for the school's problems. It's like being a referee!

Shing: A *ling* needs judges, too, An. You would be a great judge.

Shen: One day when I was waiting in your inner courtyard, Shing, I heard your father talking about a plan for our city.

Shing: Father has many plans.

Hui Ying: We tease him about having a plan for a plan!

Ancient Civilizations Reader's Theater © 2004 Creative Teaching Press

Shen: The plan he was working on that day was one to prepare for famine in our city.

Lok: Oh no, famine! Nothing to eat? That makes me very unhappy.

Shen: But, Lok, Mr. Chen's plan stores grains and other foods in case our crops are destroyed by bad weather or an earthquake.

Lok: Oh, this is just getting worse. An earthquake!

Shing: Lok, listen. A ling must help his people in good and bad times. Now we have plenty to eat and there hasn't been an earthquake in years.

Mengnu: Don't worry, if there's an earthquake we'll know and we'll send food immediately to that part of the empire.

Lok: How would we know?

An: Did you learn about the new invention for detecting earthquakes?

Lok: Ummm. I don't think so—it's not a happy thing.

An: We can't stop earthquakes, but we can help others if there is one.

Shen: I would like to make sure that storerooms are full of food for emergencies. I am organized and practical.

Lok: I would like everyone to be happy!

All the Children: Yes! We all want to be happy!

Jian: What would you like to do, Hui Ying?

Ho: Yes, do you like calligraphy or paintings? Or poetry?

Hui Ying: Like Jian, I love math, but not for building. I like taxes.

All the Children (except Hui Ying): What? Taxes? How can you like taxes?

Hui Ying: Taxes help with all the things we've talked about: schools, judges, courts, food for emergencies, bridges, new roads, enforcing laws. You can't do any of those things without taxes.

Shing: Ummm. Very, very interesting, sister.

Narrator 1: As the children continue to walk to school, they are quiet while thinking of their future choices.

Ancient Civilizations Reader's Theater © 2004 Creative Teaching Press

SAVING THE SILK

Narrator 2: Suddenly, from a side alley, they hear a loud crash and people yelling. They quickly hide in a small shop courtyard, but they can still hear the voices.

Man: I told you to be careful!

Woman: I was, but somehow he followed me.

Man: He could spoil our whole plan!

Woman: He's tied up. He can't do anything.

Man: When did you notice him watching you?

Woman: After I had stolen the plans and trading lists for the Silk Road, I saw him spying on me in the office. Then he followed me.

Man: We must keep him quiet until after we rob the trading caravan.

Woman: According to the plans, the goods going out are gold and silk—the best, most valuable of the empire's silk.

Man: If we mess up this robbery, then we'll be in prison forever! Do you understand?

Woman: Nothing will come between us and our new rich life!

Man: Give me the plans and lists. Meet me at the Red Dragon at midnight when we put our plan into action. Don't be late!

Woman: What about him? This public official who followed me?

Man: There's a shed with a lock down at the end of this alley. No one's around . . . by the time anyone finds him, we'll be living like kings!

Narrator 1: After the thieves lock up the Emperor's worker, they hurry out of the alley and down the street.

Narrator 2: The children, who have overheard everything, run to the locked shed. They are unable to unlock it, but they tell the man inside that they will return with help. They return to Mr. Chen to tell him what they heard.

Chen Long: You children are good citizens. Return to school now. Here are notes for the teachers so you won't get into trouble for being late.

Chen Lei: All of you are invited to come here directly after school.

Narrator 1: The children return to school. Much later, when school is finished for the day, they return home.

Ancient Civilizations Reader's Theater © 2004 Creative Teaching Press

SAVING THE SILK

Chen Long: Children, here is the honorable Han Wu Ti, Emperor of the Han Dynasty, Great Warrior, Defender of the People.

Wu Ti: Please, I am not much older than these young people. Call me Wu Ti.

All the Children: Oh, most honored guest, we welcome you! We wish you a long and healthy life and reign.

Wu Ti: I thank you one thousand times for your help today.

Proverb Speakers: "Nothing can compare with one act of kindness."

Wu Ti: You have solved the mystery of the missing information about the Silk Road. How can I reward each one of you?

Mengnu: May I go tonight to capture these evil thieves?

Wu Ti: No. These villains are very dangerous. Your reward will be that one day you will serve as an Imperial Guard.

Jian: Oh, most honored one, I want to learn math because someday I will build bridges and roads for the empire.

Wu Ti: This is an unusual request. My tutor will help you.

Jian: Your tutor?

Wu Ti: Yes, come to the palace every afternoon for your math lessons.

Ho: I want to learn about laws and how to make people keep them.

An: And I want to be a judge. I think Ho and I could work together.

Wu Ti: Your reward will be to learn all about laws and people. If you learn well, you will serve the empire. What do you think, Chen Long?

Chen Long: These young people will make honorable citizens.

Shing: Wu Ti, I would like to be a *ling* just like my father.

Wu Ti: It is possible. There are a lot of things to learn, but you are already on your way. Work hard. Learn about everything. Your reward will come.

Chen Lei: Daughter, you have not spoken.

Hui Ying: I like money.

Ancient Civilizations Reader's Theater © 2004 Creative Teaching Press

Everyone Else: (laughing) We all like money!

Hui Ying: Oh, I like how taxes help people to have a good life by providing jobs and improving our neighborhoods. Could I collect taxes?

Wu Ti: I understand. I know you would be an honest tax collector. Today, you all have saved the empire from danger. The good thing . . .

Lok: Good thing? This has been a sad, sad day. A man is tied, gagged, and locked up. Did you forget about the plot to rob you and your people? Sad.

Wu Ti: In all of the excitement, I forgot to say that my worker who was tied up has been rescued. He is fine. My soldiers will be waiting at the Red Dragon at midnight. All is well.

Lok: Oh, that's good. The only reward I want is for everyone to be happy!

Wu Ti: Everyone will receive rewards, but listen:

Proverb Speakers: "Your journey is the reward."

Everyone: Let's all enjoy our life and be happy! Hooray!

RELATED LESSON

Chinese Proverb Robes

OBJECTIVE

Translate a Chinese proverb and design a Chinese robe.

ACTIVITY

After the class reads and discusses the script, return to the proverbs included throughout the script. Have students discuss the meaning of the proverbs. Then, divide the class into pairs, and give each pair a **Chinese Proverb Robe reproducible (page 79).** Assign each pair one of the following Chinese proverbs to explain:

- An ant may well destroy a whole dam.
- A book holds a house of gold.
- Crows everywhere are equally black.
- A dish of carrot hastily cooked may still have soil uncleaned off the vegetable.
- Dismantle the bridge shortly after crossing it.
- Distant water will not help to put out a fire close at hand.
- A fall into a ditch makes you wiser.
- Flowing water never goes bad.
- How can you expect to find ivory in a dog's mouth?
- An inch of time is an inch of gold, but you can't buy that inch of time with an inch of gold.
- One cannot refuse to eat just because there is a chance of being choked.
- Only when all contribute their firewood can they build up a strong fire.
- A sly rabbit will have three openings to its den.

Tell students to write the proverb on the front of the pattern. Pairs should discuss the meaning of the proverb, agree upon a translation and write it on the reverse side of the robe pattern. Then, invite students to cut out the robe and decorate it using **markers, crayons, or colored pencils.** Have students share their proverb and translation with the class before displaying the robes on a clothesline suspended from the ceiling or a corner of the classroom. Have students use the display as a source for practicing their fluent reading skills.

Chinese Proverb Robe

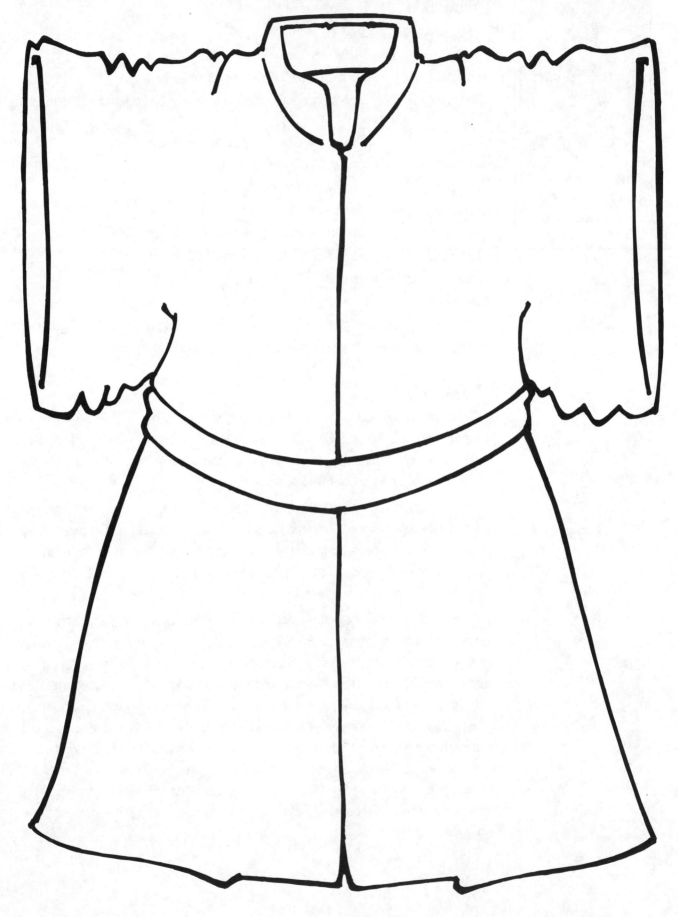

THE INDUS RIVER VALLEY PEOPLE

ANCIENT CIVILIZATIONS

VOCABULARY

Discuss each of the following words with students. Then, give clues to the definition of each word, and have students identify the correct vocabulary word.

ancient: very old; old-fashioned; relating to times long ago

decode: to change a code into ordinary language; to understand the meaning of; to read

detail: a small part of a work of art, craft, or design

enclose: to surround on all sides; close in

gag gift: a present given to someone as a joke

hypnotize: to put someone into a sleeplike state

inspire: to affect, touch, or move someone to do something

kilometer: a metric unit of length equal to 1,000 meters

masterpiece: an outstanding work of art or craft

stunning: very surprising or shocking

tradition: the passing down of ideas and culture from generation to generation

vial: a small container, usually with a lid, used for storing liquids

BACKGROUND

Cathy is excited because her Uncle Rustan is coming to see her. He is returning from a trip to India and Pakistan. Cathy and her uncle always enjoy exchanging gag gifts with each other, but sometimes weird and unpredictable things happen because of the gifts. Will the gifts cause problems for anyone this time?

From 2600 B.C. to 1900 B.C., the Indus River Valley was the site of one of the world's great urban civilizations. When the Indus River and its tributaries changed their flow patterns, the agricultural structure was disrupted, which in turn hurt the economic system. Eventually, a decline in the Indus River Valley civilization occurred. Today, this area is known as Pakistan and western India.

Within this fertile valley, well-planned cities flourished with homes that utilized brick-lined drains or underground urns for waste products from indoor bathrooms. Two cities mentioned in this play are Mohenjo-Daro, a city of 40,000 people, and Harrapa, a city of 20,000 people. Both were inhabited by craftsmen who produced useful and decorative objects. Inscribed square seals, used as identification, were made out of beautifully carved stone and engraved with five to seven symbols and animals, with the unicorn being the most common animal figure. Mystery surrounds the symbols as they remain undecipherable. Small terra cotta statues were as plentiful as the seals. In this play, the reaction caused by the bonding of the clay from the statue and the stone chips is imaginary. Of course, Uncle Rustan, Cathy, and Zach's time travel was invented as well.

PARTS

Narrator 1
Narrator 2
Chris: shop owner
Cathy: 11-year-old girl, sister to Zach
Zach: 10-year-old boy, brother to Cathy
Kate: mother of Cathy and Zach
Russell: father of Cathy and Zach
Rustan: uncle of Cathy and Zach
Uma (bright): mother of Bha, Sarama, and Arun
Bha (star): 10-year-old daughter of Uma and Sanjiv
Sarama (quick): 12-year-old daughter of Uma and Sanjiv
Arun (sun): 9-year-old son of Uma and Sanjiv
Sanjiv (long life): father of Bha, Sarama, and Arun

FLUENCY INSTRUCTION

Have students discuss the ages of the characters to help them reflect the maturity level in their reading. When you read aloud the script for students, have them listen for the following:

- Zach's imaginary words are emphasized by him and by the other speakers who pick up his words. The other speakers are humoring Zach, and Zach likes to use them to get attention. He would not want anyone to miss his new words. Model drawing out each "Zachism" as in **Zach:** *I think it's so* **strove***!*

- As a group, the children speak more quickly than the two adults.

- Changing the words that receive emphasis in a sentence can change the meaning. Have volunteers experiment with reading the line **Sanjiv:** *If the seal and statue are held by one person, and* **if** *the people gathered are honest friends, then unusual things will happen.* Emphasize the words *one, person,* and *honest* to see how it subtly changes the meaning of the line.

COMPREHENSION

After you read aloud the script, ask students these questions:

1. Why did Cathy and Zach stop at the Junk to Treasure shop on their way home from school?

2. Were Cathy and Zach looking forward to Uncle Rustan's visit? Tell why or why not.

3. How did Cathy, Zach, and Uncle Rustan get transported back to the Indus River Valley?

4. In the story, Zach liked to make up new words. Invent a new word for something ordinary, and then draw a picture of it.

5. Would you like to have an uncle like Uncle Rustan? Tell why or why not.

UNUSUAL GIFTS

Narrator 1: As Cathy and Zach walk home from school, they stop at one of Cathy's favorite shops, Junk to Treasure.

Chris: Hey, Cathy and Zach! I haven't seen you in awhile.

Cathy: Yes, we had end of school tests, but now we're done!

Zach: What's new around here? Any new treasures? Maybe we'll find another ancient coin around here.

Chris: The back room is full of unusual items. I could sure use your help over the summer. Will you have some time?

Cathy and Zach: Yes, we do! Great!

Cathy: Tonight, Uncle Rustan returns from India and Pakistan.

Chris: As usual, you need a gag gift for him. You and your uncle have an odd tradition. He manages to give you gifts that put you in danger. Like the time he gave you the toy top that sang in ancient words as it spun—and hypnotized everyone.

Zach: I've memorized the words to the song. Want to hear?

Cathy and Chris: *No!*

Chris: And the beaded necklace? When you put it on, it choked you.

Zach: I think it's so *strove*!

Cathy and Chris: *Strove?* What's that?

Zach: It means groovy, cool. I just made it up! You know I love words.

Cathy: *Strove* or not, I need something unusual. Where can I look?

Chris: You might find something in the boxes in back.

UNUSUAL GIFTS

Zach: I'll help you look, Cathy. Junk inspires me to think of new words.

Narrator 2: Later, Cathy reappears with a rectangular box.

Cathy: Look, Chris, I love this box, but I can't get it open. It's stuck.

Chris: I'll pry it open. It's lovely with small pieces of gems on the top.

Cathy: I hear something rolling around inside. Where did you get this?

Chris: From a couple who had traveled all over the world. Oomph! It was just stuck! Here, Cathy.

Cathy: Wow! Look at the details on this tiny statue.

Zach: *Zowker-Wowker!* Other than its size, it looks real!

Chris: Whoever carved this, carved a masterpiece. They even put carved jewelry on the statue!

Cathy: This is perfect for my uncle. Maybe he'll know about its history.

Narrator 1: Cathy and Zach arrive at their apartment just as their parents do. As everyone talks about their day, they prepare for Uncle Rustan's visit.

Narrator 2: For years, Cathy and her uncle have exchanged odd gifts. Now it is a family tradition.

Kate: Did you find something for Uncle Rustan, Cathy?

Zach: Did she ever! *Zowker-Wowker!* She found a lovely box with a small perfect statue inside.

Russell: And there's nothing that can go wrong, right?

Cathy: Oh, Dad. I've never given a gift that I *knew* would cause problems.

Zach: Yes, Dad. Those things just happen.

Kate: But why to only Uncle Rustan and Cathy?

Russell: Maybe it's time to stop this gift giving. The last time . . .

Kate: Ugh! The stinky red fog poured out of that Egyptian vial. It wasn't too bad until it surrounded us and made it impossible for us to move. That was bad!

Russell: What about the fierce African mask that hunted us?

Zach: What a *kinbopper* experience! Want me to do the hunt dance?

All (except Zach): No!

Ancient Civilizations Reader's Theater © 2004 Creative Teaching Press

Narrator 1: The doorbell rings, announcing Uncle Rustan's arrival. Everyone visits and catches up on the news.

Uncle Rustan: I have something special for Zach and Cathy.

Zach: *Zowker-Wowker!* A new word book on ancient languages! Thanks!

Kate: Rustan, many gifts you and Cathy have traded have had odd results.

Russell: Maybe the gifts should stop before someone is injured.

Uncle Rustan: Sometimes things just happen—no matter what we do.

Russell: I thought he'd say that!

Uncle Rustan: Here, Cathy. I can't imagine this will get us into trouble. Nothing spins, nothing moves, nothing opens.

Cathy: It's as small as a postage stamp, Unk, with writing and a picture of a unicorn on it! Wow!

Uncle Rustan: This stone seal was made over 5,000 years ago in the Indus River Valley by a master craftsman. We can't decode the writing, but all seals have different animals and writing on them.

Kate: What were they used for?

Uncle Rustan: The seals stamped wet clay, which closed pots.

Cathy: Like a safety seal that we have on our food jars today?

Zach: And to show who owned certain items?

Russell: Or to identify whose trading goods sold in another country?

Uncle Rustan: You're all right. I thought this seal most unusual because of the unicorn! I hope it's too small to cause any problems.

Cathy: Here's your gift, Unk. Just an old—but beautiful—statue.

Zach: That's amazingly *strove*!

Uncle Rustan: The Indus people made few large works of art. They seemed to like little things, like this statue and the small seals.

Kate: Russell and I have things to do. We'll see you later.

Narrator 2: Uncle Rustan holds the seal in his right hand and the statue in his left. He wants to show Cathy a special marking on the seal.

Ancient Civilizations Reader's Theater © 2004 Creative Teaching Press

Unusual Gifts

Uncle Rustan: Cathy, look here. Oh, it's getting warm . . .

Zach: That's not all! *Gadlonkers!* We're somewhere else!

Cathy: Oh-oh! We're in trouble now!

Uncle Rustan: This looks like the Indus River Valley only greener. The houses are different and . . . we're in a different time!

Cathy: No one is paying any attention to us.

Uncle Rustan: Ummm. They can't hear or see us. But listen . . .

Uma: Whether you like it or not we are moving!

Bha: I won't move! Especially to a city half the size of this one.

Uma: Father accepted a wonderful job as master of seals in Harappa. We move tomorrow. In two weeks, we'll be in our new house.

Arun: Tell us about our new city and house, Father.

Sanjiv: Our new city of 20,000 people is 200 kilometers from here. The city has more land than any other city.

Uma: Our house is on a lovely, wide street with lots of trees and it has two floors with an indoor bathroom. From our yard, you can see the Indus River.

Sanjiv: Other craftsmen and their families live on our street.

Bha: We won't know anyone. We'll have no friends. Nothing.

Sanjiv: There are more children in the new neighborhood than here. In fact, they've sent something for each of you.

Arun, Bha, and Sarama: Something for us? What? Why?

Uma: They wanted you to feel welcomed before you arrived.

Sanjiv: Here! They sent Arun a board game and dice.

Arun: Wow! This is so special. What a welcome!

Uma: Bha and Sarama, other new friends sent you these small statues.

Bha: Oh my. These are perfect! Look at the jewelry on them!

Sarama: These are works of art. Gorgeous.

Ancient Civilizations Reader's Theater © 2004 Creative Teaching Press

UNUSUAL GIFTS

Cathy: Look! The one that Bha has is the one I bought you, Unk.

Uncle Rustan: So it is. How odd.

Arun, Bha, and Sarama: Let's make gifts for our new friends.

Sanjiv: So it's okay to move?

Bha, Sarama, Arun: Yes! We'll try our best.

Sanjiv: Your new friends will treasure a well-made seal. Let's get to work!

Narrator 1: Sanjiv and his family go into their workshop. The children carve small postage stamp–size stone seals.

Zach: *Wizzurkos!* These kids are wonders!

Cathy: Uncle Rustan, look at Bha's seal.

Uncle Rustan: The unicorn seal that I gave you! Amazing!

Narrator 2: Bha scrapes clay from the statue and mixes it with stone chips from the seal. Then she puts the mixture on the statue and the seal.

Bha: Father, I've tied the statue and seal together. My new friend and I will be tied in friendship just as the statue and seal are.

Sanjiv: *If* the seal and statue are held by one person, and *if* the people gathered are honest friends, then unusual things will happen.

Uncle Rustan: What an honor to see all of this!

Zach: But, Unk, how do we get back? Like into the 21st century!

Cathy: Ummm. I'll hold the seal.

Narrator 1: Suddenly, Uncle Rustan, Cathy, and Zach are back in the apartment. Kate and Russell come into the room.

Kate: Thank goodness nothing's happened. No fog, hunting, or ancient music or words. No one being choked. No one disappearing. Whew!

Russell: I guess the gifts are ordinary this year. What a relief!

Uncle Rustan, Cathy, Zach: That's right. Nothing unusual. Just your normal, ordinary gifts.

Zach: It is so *strove* to be us! *Zowker-Wowker!*

Ancient Civilizations Reader's Theater © 2004 Creative Teaching Press

RELATED LESSON

Artifact Prediction Box

OBJECTIVES

Predict and record the significance of objects within the script before reading, actively listen for a specific purpose, and check predictions after reading the script.

ACTIVITY

Begin by collecting and storing in a **small box or bag** the following objects: **small sign that reads "Junk to Treasure," small map of India and Pakistan, small wrapped gift, spinning toy top, beaded necklace, small statue, plastic food container lid/seal, picture of a unicorn, book,** and **dice.** Prepare the chart shown below:

Object	Predicted Significance	Actual Significance
1. Junk to Treasure sign		
2. maps		
3. gift		
4. toy top		
5. beaded necklace		
6. statue		
7. seal		
8. unicorn		
9. book		
10. dice		

Begin by telling students that they are about to read a script titled *Unusual Gifts*. Explain that you will show them ten items from the script and they are to predict what part each will play in the story. Show each item, one at a time, and record students' predictions on the chart under the "Predicted Significance" column. After students have finished making their predictions, tell them that they should listen carefully to the story in order to discover the actual significance of each item. After reading the script, return to the prediction chart, and ask students to either confirm or modify their predictions accordingly.

THE MESOPOTAMIANS

ANCIENT CIVILIZATIONS

VOCABULARY

Discuss each of the following words with students. Then, choose one of the words from the list. Invite students to ask up to 10 yes/no questions in order to attempt to discover the word. Explain that students may try to identify the word at any time before ten questions have been asked. After each word is identified, repeat the activity with a new word.

ex-con: a person who was once a criminal

papyrus: a kind of paper made by ancient Egyptians

perk: an extra benefit from a person's place of work

pickled: food, such as a cucumber, that is preserved in salt water or a vinegar solution

scribe: a secretary or writer, especially in ancient times

tend: to take care of; watch over; look after

tourism: traveling for pleasure

uprising: a revolt or rebellion

BACKGROUND

Mesopotamia, "the flat land between the rivers," is often referred to as the "cradle of civilization." Its fertile land supported several thousand people, first as the empire of Sumer and later as the empire of Babylonia. Today, this land between the Tigris and Euphrates Rivers in western Asia is known as Iraq.

Hammurabi, the best-known Amorite ruler, who ruled from about 1792 B.C.–1750 B.C., expanded Babylon from a city-state to the capital of the kingdom of Babylonia. Not much is known about his family life, although his first son was Samsuiluna, nicknamed Sam for this play, who succeeded his father as ruler of Babylonia.

Hammurabi is well known for his set of 282 laws, which were based on economic, family, criminal, and civil law, with an emphasis on justice and consistency. His practical improvements such as irrigation systems, tax reforms, and use of natural resources, government housing, and trade with neighbors indicate that Babylon would have been a safe and attractive place to live and work. Craftsmen, soldiers, farmers, boat builders, traders, inventors, and textile weavers contributed to the success of the Babylonian Empire. The use of the water clock, 12-month calendar, wheel, plow, sailboat, and other inventions improved daily life for the Mesopotamian inhabitants. Scribes were important in record keeping, and *edubbas* were Sumerian scribe schools. Astronomers were special scribes who recorded observations of the stars and planets and advised the king about what to do and when to do it. No records indicate that Hammurabi conducted a public relations campaign for tourism and new workers, but the importance and success of fishing, farming, metalworking, weaving, trading, rivers, and waterways would have made Babylon an attractive location for additional craftsmen and tourists.

The Babylonian dynasty was ended by attacks by the Hittites, who are mentioned in the play as being unattractive for tourists by Hammurabi, which is a fabrication.

PARTS

Narrator
Hammurabi: King of Babylon
Lugal (big man): mayor of Babylon
Aya: chief of advertising for Babylon
Erishti: advertising worker
Samsuiluna: nicknamed "Sam,"
    12-year-old son of Hammurabi
Inanna (gentle): 11-year-old friend
    of Sam
Deborah (to speak kind words):
    10-year-old friend of Sam
The Candy Wrappers: a rap group

FLUENCY INSTRUCTION

Have students discuss the ages of the characters to help them reflect the maturity level in their reading. When you read aloud the script for students, have them listen for the following:

- An ellipsis signals a longer than usual pause as in the line *Aya: Yes . . . but why is that important to tourists?*
- An ellipsis may also signal where one reader ends a line and another reader begins it as in the lines *Aya: Today we'll uncover two projects. One, to bring tourists into Babylon and . . . Erishti: . . . Two, to bring workers into our growing kingdom.*
- The Candy Wrappers rap all their lines. It is okay to subtly emphasize some of the rimes, but in general, the reader should emphasize the meaning of the line over the rime. Read some of the Candy Wrappers' lines to show students how to read beyond the punctuation.

COMPREHENSION

After you read aloud the script, ask students these questions:

1. How does Hammurabi, the King of Babylon, plan to attract workers and visitors to his kingdom?

2. In what other ways could people be encouraged to work in or visit Babylon?

3. Identify three advantages of working in Babylon. Identify three advantages of vacationing in Babylon.

4. Name several modern-day inventions that include the concept of the wheel in their design.

5. Which of the inventions mentioned in the script made the greatest impact on life at that time? Support your answer with examples.

LAND BETWEEN THE RIVERS

PARTS

Narrator
Hammurabi: King of Babylon
Lugal (big man): mayor of Babylon
Aya: chief of advertising for Babylon
Erishti: advertising worker
Samsuiluna: nicknamed "Sam,"
   12-year-old son of Hammurabi
Inanna (gentle): 11-year-old friend
   of Sam
Deborah (to speak kind words):
   10-year-old friend of Sam
The Candy Wrappers: a rap group

Narrator: The King of Babylon wants to bring new workers to the kingdom and to increase tourism.

Hammurabi: I need more workers. In addition, I want Babylon to be a vacation spot.

Lugal: That's why we asked the experts in advertising to come today.

Aya: Thanks for calling our office. I understand what you want us to do. I'll handle the vacation advertising.

Erishti: I'll take care of the new workers.

Aya: Maybe the rap group the Candy Wrappers could do a rap about Babylon. They recently did an ad for the new water clock. Listen.

The Candy Wrappers:

Sun's out today. You're feeling okay. Tending your herd, free as a bird.
Night comes along. You sing a song. You head for bed, you sleepyhead.
No sun this day. It's dark and gray. Can't move from bed. Cows not fed.
The herd is sad. They feel so bad. What do they do? Buy something new.
A water clock. There's no ticktock. Does it need sun? No! It needs none.
It measures time, anytime! No sun this day. It's dark and gray.
Herd is not sad. The farmer is glad. What's new on the block?
The water clock! It saves the day! Hip, hip hooray!

Sam: Great! I bet it caught people's attention.

Erishti: It sure did! We'll do a rap for working in and visiting Babylon.

Aya: Who will see the ads?

Lugal: We want all of our neighbors to hear about our vacation spots.

Hammurabi: Include Egypt and Greece. I don't want the Hittites to come here on vacation. They are always trying to take over our kingdom.

Aya:	Why would people want to vacation here?
Hammurabi:	My son Sam and his friends will tell you about that.
Sam:	For tourists our big draw is water!
Aya:	Water?
Sam:	Yea. We're the land between two rivers, the Tigris and the Euphrates.
Aya:	Yes . . . but why is that important to tourists?
Deborah:	Water sports!
Sam:	We have rafts, sailboats, round reed boats, and large boats. Visitors can run the rapids and wind surf. They can tour the river on a river boat.
Deborah:	Maybe we can build a water park with slides, tubing, and so on.
Inanna:	People could camp out on an island.
Aya:	Camp out?
Sam:	Most people have their own tents. We give them a new location.
Aya:	Oh. Anything else?
Sam:	We have hot, dry weather from spring to fall so it's a three-season hit. Any other ideas, Inanna?
Inanna:	Sure. Food. Fancy meals could be part of the river boat trip. Picnics could be offered for hikers and campers. The kingdom could start its own fast-food chain, Grab and Eat.
Aya:	Any ideas for highlighting a special food?
Inanna:	We have lots of fish. Fish can be dried, pickled, salted, or served fresh. A menu can be built around fish.
Aya:	Anying else? [pause] Then Erishti will take over.
Erishti:	Let's talk about the second part of your goal. Why would people want to work in Babylon?
Lugal:	We have so many interesting jobs.
Erishti:	Like what?
Lugal:	We have jobs for astronomers.

Ancient Civilizations Reader's Theater © 2004 Creative Teaching Press

Erishti: What do they do?

Lugal: They study the stars and planets.

Erishti: Easy enough.

Lugal: Then they advise the king on what to do or not do on certain days.

Hammurabi: I might want to do something in the month of Ululu. I check with my astronomers. They might say, "No! If you do that, there will be an uprising against you."

Deborah: Oh-oh!

Hammurabi: Another time, I might have good luck. The astronomers tell me when I am in danger or not.

Deborah: Whew!

Hammurabi: It is important to have the best astronomers.

Erishti: I understand. Are there other jobs?

Lugal: We need metalworkers and craftspeople, especially those who carve valuable stones. We import a lot of wood, so we need woodworkers.

Hammurabi: Our weavings are the best in the world. We need salespeople to sell our cloth in other kingdoms.

Sam: I think curious people would like to live here.

Erishti: Curious?

Sam: If they're curious, they could be inventors. After all, we are the inventors of the wheel, the plow, and the sailboat.

The Candy Wrappers: And the water clock!

Erishti: Okay. Any other kinds of workers?

Hammurabi, Lugal, Sam, and Inanna: Many more!

Deborah: My family moved here four years ago. My father is a teacher.

Erishti: I can add teachers to the list.

Deborah: You could, but I'm making another point. He teaches in an edubbas, a school for boys. Students work hard from early morning until evening. After 12 years of school, they could be scribes for the king.

Ancient Civilizations Reader's Theater © 2004 Creative Teaching Press

LAND BETWEEN THE RIVERS

Sam: Families already move here so their sons can become scribes.

Erishti: Ummm. Anything else?

Hammurabi: Yes, a smart reason to move here is our code of laws. Babylon is a safe place to live and to raise a family.

Lugal: Here's a copy of Hammurabi's 282 laws.

Aya: Is there one that is more important than another?

Hammurabi: My laws deal with family, slavery, trading, fields, and trees.

Sam: People often talk about "an eye for an eye, and a tooth for a tooth."

Erishti: You're right. Everyone knows that one!

Aya: If that's all, we'll return to our office. We'll see you next week with our ideas.

Narrator: A week later, everyone gathers to hear ideas about tourists and workers.

Aya: Today we'll uncover two projects. One, to bring tourists into Babylon and . . .

Erishti: . . . Two, to bring workers into our growing kingdom.

Aya: For both goals, we will contact other lands.

Sam: Perfect.

Aya: "Work and Play in the Land Between the Rivers" will be our slogan.

Erishti: We'll build billboards along roads and waterways.

Aya: We'll send scribes to other cities. They'll announce benefits of living in or visiting Babylon.

Erishti: Traders going to Egypt will bring back papyrus. We'll use the papyrus for travel brochures.

Aya: Artists will paint posters and banners to hang in public places.

Erishti: We'll advertise for farmers, craftspeople, inventors, and scientists. I didn't forget about cooks, salespeople, and boat builders.

Sam: Life guards, sailing instructors, and camping leaders, too.

Aya: We can add those.

Inanna: Let's set up travel offices in other lands!

Ancient Civilizations Reader's Theater © 2004 Creative Teaching Press

LAND BETWEEN THE RIVERS

Lugal: Great idea!

Hammurabi: We'll stamp a special king's seal on any advertising.

Inanna: It will mean, "This is the king's project!"

Lugal: Okay. The Indus people have seals, but they're small. The Minoans have larger ones.

Hammurabi: Send traders to Phoenicia. They'll find a Minoan seal there.

Sam: What else?

Erishti: We'll highlight our safe kingdom.

Hammurabi: Good. Good.

Erishti: We have a rap. If you like it, we could use it all over the world. People would know about opportunities here. Here's the rap group!

The Candy Wrappers: We call this rap "Work and Play."
Choose a place with lots of work, a place that has more than one perk,
A place of sun and little rain, a land of rivers and great grain.
Babylon, Babylon, with great laws and no ex-cons.
Hammurabi is quite a king. His laws are fair, but they can sting.
"An eye for an eye, a tooth for a tooth." You're in trouble when he finds the truth.
If you want a puppet on a string, Hammurabi's not the right king.
If you're looking for a family place, Babylon will win the race!
Come as well to camp and explore. Swim and boat from shore to shore.
You'll eat well from day to night, fish and fruit and breads delight.
If you're looking for a job to do, we have one that's right for you.
You'll have a choice of two or three, carve stones or wood of a big pine tree.
If you like to invent or weave, from Babylon you'll never leave.
Babylon, where friends can blend and work together until the end.

Ancient Civilizations Reader's Theater © 2004 Creative Teaching Press

RELATED LESSON

Babylon Travel Brochure

OBJECTIVES

Recall information from the script about ancient Babylon, research information on ancient Babylon using a variety of sources, construct an ancient Babylonia concept cluster, and create a travel brochure for ancient Babylonia.

ACTIVITY

After reading and discussing the script with students, have the class brainstorm a list of concepts students learned from the script about the ancient Babylonian civilization. List these on the board, and discuss them. Divide the class into small groups of three to four students, and ask them to research additional information about Babylon. Add this information to the list on the board, and correct any misinformation previously offered. Then, give each student a **Babylonian Cluster graphic organizer (page 96).** Have students write *Ancient Babylonia* in the center circle. Ask students to review the list of brainstormed concepts and note similarities among items. Have them combine similar terms into short lists, and create appropriate subheadings. Ask students to write the subheadings in the circles nearest the center topic circle and cluster the other words around the corresponding headers.

After students complete the cluster, tell them that they are to assume they have been hired by King Hammurabi to design a travel brochure that will encourage people to work in or visit his kingdom. Share **samples of travel brochures from other states and countries** with students. Call their attention to the layout, design, and content of the brochures. Have students work individually, in pairs, or in small groups. Give students a **sheet of drawing paper,** and have them fold it into thirds. Encourage them to use the information they wrote in the cluster to create their travel brochure. Explain that the brochure should contain these features:

- the name of the location (ancient Babylon)
- hand-drawn or computer-generated illustrations such as maps, scenes, or logos
- useful information for visitors such as geographic location, historical information, city map, things to do/activities, things to see, where to eat/food, landmarks, places to stay, form of government, forms of available transportation, employment opportunities, and climate

Encourage students to make rough drafts of their brochure before they create their final draft. Invite students to share the brochures before you display them in the classroom.

Babylonian Cluster

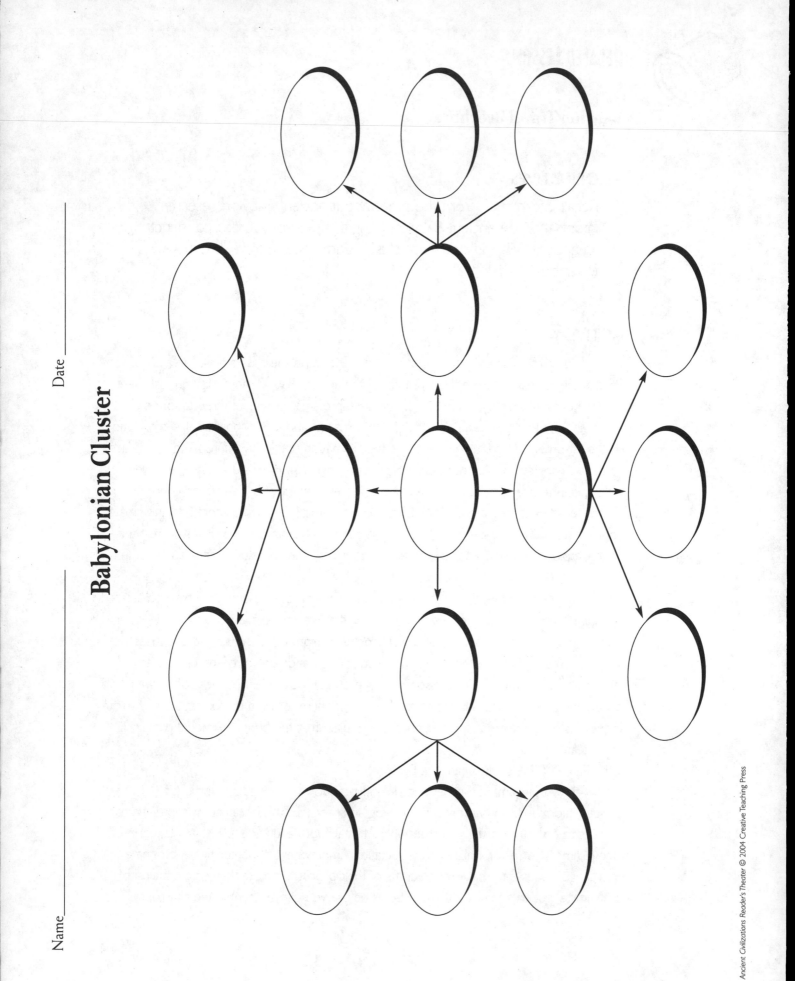